AMERICA'S LITERARY REVOLT

AMERICA'S
LITERARY REVOLT

By

MICHAEL YATRON

Essay Index Reprint Series

BOOKS FOR LIBRARIES PRESS
FREEPORT, NEW YORK

STANDARD BOOK NUMBER:

8369-1437-6

LIBRARY OF CONGRESS CATALOG CARD NUMBER:

70-99653

PRINTED IN THE UNITED STATES OF AMERICA

To my wife Georgine
who served as my typist and inspiration

TABLE OF CONTENTS

AMERICA'S LITERARY REVOLT

Chapter I

Populism

Today, past the turn of the midcentury, there is a feeling that something has gone wrong, that the American dream has been perverted. We know vaguely that this is the natural result of industrialization and urbanization, of advanced technology and a growing population, but only one movement of the American scene that we can give a name to, Populism, can offer some explanation as to what has gone wrong and indicate what America might have been. This movement which reflected the yearnings of the common man, often contradictory, came out of the West, the area from which so much of the best in American democracy has come.

It had many part-time spokesmen: one need only mention Frank Norris, Hamlin Garland, Theodore Dreiser, and Sherwood Anderson. But its most consistent spokesmen were Edgar Lee Masters, Vachel Lindsay, and Carl Sandburg, three friends, each a product of the same time and place, each giving voice to the same sentiments, without realizing often that they were rebels bound to the same cause. Thus it is not strange that literary critics, concentrating on what they thought to be unique in each man, have seen Masters as a village cynic, Lindsay as a naive jazz poet, and Sandburg as the bard of steel and stockyards.

If, on reading these pages, these rebels seem to have been foolish men, trying to hold back time and change, one need only reflect that Aristotle believed that any state with a population in excess of 10,000 was undesirable, that Jefferson opposed the mobs of the cities, and that unrestricted population growth has vulgarized every aspect of life and transformed human life everywhere to resemble that of the beehive and the anthill.

The word *Populism* presents a difficulty at the outset because it permits of no exact definition. Even the origin of the term is uncertain, and while the Populist Party of the 1890's and the early 1900's was inspired by economic depression, Populism itself had much wider implications, implications which transcended both politics and economics. Populism expressed a way of life that was in opposition to the major developments taking place in a rapidly changing America. It was a way of life characterized by simplicity, hard work, honesty, thrift, and value of the product in terms of toil and time rather than in monetary terms. Accordingly, the new captains of industry and finance were not viewed as titans worthy of admiration. Rather they were seen as leeches, parasites feeding on the lifeblood of other men's toil, merchants of death summed up by the phrase *Wall Street*.

The ascendancy of Wall Street in the American economy interested the Populists in the mystery of money and its manipulations, for they were sure that Wall Street controlled money values to the detriment of the wage earners' standard of living. This is not to say that the Populist's were anti-capitalist or Socialist, but rather that they were as hostile to Wall Street bankers and industrialists as the Socialists themselves.

Nevertheless the Populists were often identified as Socialists, and were even accused of being anarchists, charges which they strenuously denied. Charles Q. De France, Secretary of the People's Party (National Committee), complained as late as May, 1905, in *Tom Watson's Magazine*, the main voice of Populism:

> Populism is a term at which many eminently respectable but sadly misinformed persons shy. . . . They regard it as synonymous with Socialism, anarchy, bomb-throwing, nihilism and half a dozen other real or fancied evils. . . . Populism is neither socialism nor anarchism. It is neither

idealistic nor materialistic. It is neither collectivistic nor individualistic. It is essentially eclectic.

It is precisely this eclecticism which makes Populism a loose complex of ideas, only a few of which are positive, the large majority being negative. Thus an expanded description of Populism as a revolutionary political credo and as a reactionary literary movement is necessary.

Political Populism had its roots in the growth of the American economy after the Civil War, in the rapid settlement of the West, and in the end of the frontier. Instrumental in this rapid settlement were the railroads, which, eager to expand, not only advertised the advantages of settling in the West, but offered all sorts of inducements to settlers. The results were boom-towns and a mushrooming of villages. The railroads profited by this movement of population, but not the settlers who had been enticed into the West. These victims of a "boom or bust" psychology soon glutted the market with their agricultural products. The immediate and long term results were depressed prices.

Along with the settlement of the West came changes in methods of agriculture and manufacture. Machinery rapidly increased farm production. The fall in prices thus engendered brought the farmers together for mutual protection and with the intention of taking concerted action to preserve and improve their position. Thus there came into existence the Grange of 1867, the Agricultural Wheel of 1878, and the Farmers' Alliance of 1879. These and similar organizations were the forerunners of the People's Party.

Inevitably, the farmers and their supporters contrasted their economically depressed state with the relative prosperity of the East. The point of view was developed that it was the plutocrats of the East, and of Wall Street in particular, who had gained control of the Government, and who were running it to serve their own interests. And before long, the farmers began to look back longingly to the "good old days" of the pre-Civil War period when they had had the advantages of a more stable agrarian economy and a smaller population. Edgar Lee Masters expressed in the November, 1906, issue of *Tom Watson's Magazine* what had become a nostalgia for them:

> Fifty years ago there was less wealth, but there was also less poverty. There were fewer railroads. There were no telephones, and men were compelled to improve their memories for the occasion to speak. People stayed at home and laid the foundations for the nation's wealth. The great cities were few, industry was decentralized, and competition was a real fact. The states were sovereign. . . .

The farmers, while convinced that their lack of prosperity was directly due to the low prices they received for their produce, also believed that the more currency there was in circulation the happier everyone would be. This conviction led them to organize the "Greenbacker" political party of the 1870's to agitate for a cheaper currency. Feeling that they were the victims of a deliberate policy of deflation, they identified their enemy as the banker of the East, who circulated his own notes—in competition with the Federal Government's issuance of Greenbacks—and earned compound interest on them.

The 1880's, the decade in which the Farmers' Alliances reached their peak of importance, was a period of intellectual and social ferment. As Anne Rochester said of those years, "Thoughts and theories sprouted like weeds after a May shower." In 1879 appeared Henry George's *Progress and Poverty*. In 1881 came Henry Demarest Lloyd's exposure of Standard Oil, and, seven years later, Edward Bellamy's *Looking Backward*. There were also labor strikes, one of which exploded into the Haymarket Riot in Chicago, in 1886, and which highlighted the class struggle between wage earners and corporations. Four of the Haymarket rioters were hanged, an act which convinced the "Liberals" of the day that the police and courts had connived at a miscarriage of justice for the sake of the moneyed powers.

The political ferment brought about the defeat of the Republicans in 1884, giving the Democrats power for the first time since 1860. Then, in 1887, there was a crop failure which aroused both the Southern and Western farmers to a more concerted action. The idea of a farmers' political party or a third party, though not overtly expressed, had its inception in St. Louis, December 6, 1889. There a convention, consisting of delegates from farmers' organizations and from the Knights of Labor, effected a union of the two classes under the name of the Farmers' Alliance and Industrial Union.

On December 7, 1890, a convention was held at Ocala, Florida, attended by members of the Southern Alliance, the Farmers' Mutual Benefit Association, and the Colored Alliance. Although the third party idea remained unpronounced, the political stage was set for the establishment of the People's Party. In a convention lasting several days, the National Farmers' Alliance had worked out a body of principles and put forward a well-defined program for future action which foretold the course of independent political procedure.

The People's Party was launched in Cincinnati. The *New York Times* of May 20, 1891, reported:

> The platform is based on the Ocala platform, but contains some political measures, and a few Knights of Labor pledges, such as the eight hour day. The planks of the platform are as follows: free coinage of silver, abolition of national banks, loans on land and real estate, subtreasuries, income tax, plenty of paper money, government control of railroads, election of President, Vice-President and Senators by direct vote, non-ownership of land by foreigners, revenue of the state and nation limited to expenses, eight hours' work, and universal suffrage.

The following year, 1892, was a presidential election year, and the People's Party held their convention in Omaha, their political platform bearing the same stamp as that of the three previous conventions. General James B. Weaver of Iowa was

5

the People's Party candidate for President (caricatured by the cartoonists of the time as a "hayseed"), while General James B. Field was its candidate for Vice-President.

The election returns gave Grover Cleveland 5,556,918 popular votes and 277 Electoral Votes. Benjamin Harrison came second with 5,176,108 votes and 145 Electoral votes. James B. Weaver, however, gained 1,041,028 votes, with 22 Electoral votes. This respectable showing, coupled with the election of eight Congressmen and two Senators, revealed that the People's Party was a new political force. What is more, the Party was addressing the people through nearly 900 newspapers by the year 1892.

In 1893, a panic began in the financial world which started a prolonged industrial depression. Hundreds of banks failed, railroad construction came to a standstill, factories closed, and unemployment reached a new high level. Basic agricultural crops suffered a further decline in prices. Yet despite these economic conditions, ostensibly favorable to Populism, the movement lost ground. In the elections of 1894 the Populists were defeated in most of the Western States where, in 1892, they had enjoyed success.

In 1896 the Populists united with the Democratic Party. Since the members of the Populist Party came from the liberal rank and file of the Democratic and Republican Parties, this fusion was not difficult. The Democratic Party in its Chicago convention of 1896 was faced by a rank and file which had been aroused by the People's Party to retreat from Clevelandism and return to the principles of Jefferson, Jackson and Lincoln. Not only the platform, but the confidence-inspiring personality of the Democratic candidate, William Jennings Bryan, attracted the members of the People's Party, making them willing to fuse with the Democratic Party. Thus the People's Party lost its identity.

The defeat of Bryan brought disillusionment and lamentation among the Populists. Thomas E. Watson, Bryan's running mate, pointed out that the fusion and the defeat resulted in the demise of the People's Party paper which he had founded in Atlanta, Georgia, in 1891. The mortality among the Populist

6

newspapers, however, had another cause: the great advertisers of the land, often allied with Wall Street, refused to give them any business.

William J. Bryan, the silver-tongued orator, became *persona non grata* to the Populists. Tom Watson expressed the Populists' disillusionment and disapproval when he wrote:

> For thirteen years they (the Populists) have spoken when he has been silent. They have toiled with principles while he has been 'playing politics.' They braved public ridicule and opprobrium while he was basking on the sunny side and trumpeting for his little side-track issues of Tariff for revenue, with the incidental protection, and Free Silver.

After the election of 1896, Populism rapidly lost importance as a political movement; nevertheless, its adherents continued to see hope in every election. In spite of the fact that the election of 1904 marked the complete demise of the People's Party, they refused to admit defeat, finding encouragement in the fact that such men as William Randolph Hearst, Thomas E. Watson, Senator La Follete of Wisconsin, Governor Folk of Missouri, and William Jennings Bryan were champions of reform. In fact, Thomas E. Watson began publishing his monthly magazine, *Tom Watson's Magazine,* as late as March, 1905.

But within six months Watson knew that, as a political movement, his cause was dead. It could survive only as one of protest. With considerable insight, he insisted that Populism would continue to be a power in the land even if none of its leaders ever held office.

Literary Populists like Masters, Lindsay, and Sandburg were, in a sense, to "hold office" in the next half century but most of the people who were associated with the political Populism of the period are no longer remembered. Anne Rochester has said of the latter, "Many have achieved a pallid immortality of a paragraph in local history or in a dictionary of biography. Only a few have found a place in our common memory as living personalities." [1]

In spite of their failure as a political organization, the Populists saw many of their revolutionary ideals translated into reality. Their proposal for the Australian system of voting resulted in improved registration laws and other devices for insuring a free ballot and a fair count. Women's suffrage became a reality. United States Senators came to be elected by the direct vote of the people. The primary election became widely used for the making of party nominations. Populist free silver agitation compelled the economists to study the money question. Government warehouses for the storage of grain came into existence. Railroads, though not taken over by the government, were to be rigidly controlled by it. The eight-hour day became a reality, and labor came to enjoy a far more equitable treatment.

The shibboleths of the Middle-Western Populists were "money power," "monopoly," and "satanic mills": rallying cries which lacked positive inspiration and, therefore, purpose. The Populists readily identified their real or imagined enemies: imperialist wars, Wall Street, international bankers, and the sinister international conspiracy which had its headquarters in England. But, they lacked certainty concerning what they should support, and, more important, they lacked a coherent philosophy and the inspiration of an "ideal state," the forces which have given vitality and purpose to so many political movements.

Populism also lacked a programme. It survived only so long as the circumstances which gave it birth survived. As soon as these changed, having neither the need nor the means to link itself to new circumstances, Populism, as a political movement, perished.

Equally decisive in the disappearance of Populism was the change from an agricultural America to an industrial America. The big city replaced the American small farm as the locus of political power. In addition, technological advances in communication made the isolationism of the Middle-West anomalous even fifty years ago. In effect, Populism was the collective protest of the agrarian segment of America against changes they resented and newcomers (immigrants) whom they feared. And it was this resentment and fear that gave Populism its reactionary cast.

Populism in its literary manifestation was mainly reactionary, and by reactionary we mean that the Populists wanted to turn the clock back to a period which had ceased to exist a half a century before the election of 1896. They wanted to return to the river world of Mark Twain's *Huckleberry Finn*, to a boy's world of straw hat, bare feet, and fishing pole. On an adult level this world is characterized by small villages and farms, by hard-working stoic agrarians, who know how to live, love, work, fight—and who are thoroughly equalitarian and democratic. Nostalgia is, in a word, the essence of the reaction which runs throughout literary Populism.

Nostalgia is a universal feeling. The past, bereft of all its dangers, pains and anxieties, can be looked back on with confidence. But this nostalgia is usually tempered with an adult acceptance of change, of the inevitability of change. Nevertheless, the literary Populists, whom we are to discuss, not only cherished their nostalgias but steadfastly refused to accept the century of technological advance from 1840 to 1940.

It is this refusal to emerge from the agricultural stage of civilization to a more advanced stage that divorces these Populists from most modern liberal and utopian thought. To be sure, Populism, as the word signifies, was a "people's movement," and various Populists, writing in *Tom Watson's Magazine*, were willing to make common cause with all democratic movements and to identify themselves with efforts to abolish serfdom or to effect changes of the status quo. They hailed Mikhail Bakunin as an apostle of Populism; they rejoiced that Japan was arising from "the dust of a Buddhist serf-kennel"; and they claimed kinship to Solon and the Attic Constitution.

Yet in spite of this cosmopolitanism the movement itself was xenophobic. It was suspicious of anyone who was not a farmer, and even preferred its farmers to be of the Middle-West. It was no accident that planks in the platform of the People's Party included non-ownership of land by foreigners and

9

prohibition of immigration. For foreigners and foreign ways adulterated the old values and old mores.

The Populists extended their resentment of alien ways to include the cities, the centers where people were destined to congregate in vast numbers. They could not envision that cities might one day help ameliorate human existence, including their own, by developing many technologies. They could not see the cities as centers of culture, abounding in universities, libraries, theatres and museums. They somehow could not envision, as the Socialists and Communists have, the individual of a future Utopia, working three or four hours a day to achieve both necessities and luxuries and having leisure to enjoy the arts.

The Populists were also consistently reactionary in their *Weltanschauung* where culture and leisure were concerned. They distrusted both, they had a contempt for both, they identified both as representative of the moneyed East and of decadent, monarch-infested Europe. For the Populists virtue and manhood lay in hard physical work; higher education, high flown language, well-made clothing, good manners—these were effeminacies to be ridiculed.

One can possibly account for this Populist boorishness as a rationalization of the struggle for existence that had gone on for decades on the American frontier. Fancy clothing, fancy speech, fancy manners were of little use against Indian arrows and virgin land; they were of little use on the farmstead. But it was the wearing of this boorishness as a badge of honor that shows the depth of the Populist prejudice against "niceties" associated with class distinctions.

The newspaper and periodical cartoonists of the '90's invariably depicted Populists as "hayseeds" and "one-gallus" types. O. Henry, for example, in a humorous detective story written in 1894, "A Successful Political Intrigue," had made the fact a Populist politician was suspected of wearing socks cause of his withdrawal as a candidate. This type of derision had little effect. Lindsay and Sandburg were proud to be "hayseeds" and affected personal slovenliness throughout their lives.

10

Chapter II

EDGAR LEE MASTERS

Background for Nostalgia

Masters' lifelong nostalgia for rural America had its origin in his boyhood and youth. Every summer, from his fourteenth to his twentieth year, he visited the farm of his grandfather, Squire Davis Masters. A native of Virginia, Squire Masters acquired his first farm near Murrayville, Illinois, in 1829. In 1847 he moved to the Sangamon River country, some five miles north of Petersburg, Illinois, in the very heart of the prairie landscape. For "Lee" Masters, this country was ideal:

> The rims of forestry, the distant houses, the Mason Country Hills, the rail fences and hedges, the thunderheads, the undulating land toward the house and barn of George Kirby two miles north, all seem like a fairy world. . . .

Masters' attachment to Sangamon County was strengthened by pride of birth, which made him feel that he "belonged," that he was "American." As a lawyer of twenty-eight he asked his paternal grandmother to make out an affidavit concerning her ancestry. The fact that he was "a native son" bred in him a virulent xenophobia. Despite his democratic tendencies and essential humanitarianism, he was never quite able to accept the immigrants who swelled the American population. Unlike Sandburg, the son of immigrants, and Lindsay, a religious equalitarian, Masters did not develop an affection which em-

11

braced all the people. Industrialism and money contaminated "Spoon River," but according to Masters, the foreign invasion doomed it:

> I saw that the village names were changed;
> And instead of Churchill, Spears, and Rutledge,
> It was Schoenwald and Stefanik,
> And Berkowitz and Garnadillo
> And then I said with a sinking heart,
> Goodbye Republic, old dear!
>
> "McDowell Young"

To Masters, the grandfather who taught him pacifism also personified the pioneer of the pristine Republic and the idealism of Jeffersonian democracy. Squire Masters was a hard-working, hardy, incorruptible farmer. He was a representative man and, to Lee Masters, all that he represented was admirable —even if "old-fashioned." Though Lee believed in free-love, he was proud of Squire Masters' devotion to his wife in a marriage that lasted seventy years. Squire Masters, in fact, incarnated stability and contentment. He was what the Populists meant by the word "people," and he was destined to become a theme of Masters.

Just as Squire Masters represented an ideal, so did his wife, Lucinda Matlock, become the prototype of the American pioneer woman. She lived to the age of ninety-six, rearing twelve children and losing eight before she was sixty. Masters had her say from her grave:

> What is this I hear of sorrow and weariness,
> Anger, discontent and drooping hopes?
> Degenerate sons and daughters,
> Life is too strong for you.
> It takes life to love Life.
>
> "Lucinda Matlock"

Masters' grandparents symbolized the arcadian way of life which was being submerged by time. He idealized his grand-

12

parents and mourned that their formula for successful living was being abandoned in a changing America.

Lee's boyhood harmonized with the idea personified by his grandparents. He attended the public schools of Petersburg, a place well qualified to arouse nostalgia. Petersburg was something right out of the pages of *Tom Sawyer* and *Huckleberry Finn*:

> How often in my boyhood I cast my line
> Beneath the shadow of the Salem Mill.
> "The Old Salem Mill: Petersburg"

And Lee remained with the conviction that there was no town in Illinois more attractive than Petersburg on the Sangamon.

But with Masters the real and the present was often inferior to the vanished and the non-existent. As much as he loved Petersburg, near by New Salem (a village abandoned three decades before Masters' birth) became for him the ideal American village:

> At New Salem there were wrestling matches, horse races, footraces, and at times fist fights. But these men were a different breed from the Spoon River crowd. They were laughing, humorous, and more given to amiable delight.

In spite of his grandparents and Petersburg, Masters' mature life was tainted with pessimism. Nor could he account for this gloomy turn of mind. He wrote in his autobiography: "In the first diary that I ever kept, dating from my fifteenth year, I see no trace of myself as I grew to be along the way."

Masters records in his autobiography that his family's moving to Lewistown, Illinois, when he was eleven, was a happy event. Yet though Masters spent the next decade there, he usually wrote about his "beloved" Petersburg. One reason for his desire to forget Lewistown was that it afforded him many sore memories.

Hardin Masters, Lee's father, was a lawyer who fared badly in Lewistown. Intense legal competition, a cloudy reputation

13

of "Copperhead," and a lack of experience in business law and realty resulted in the eventual exhaustion of his financial resources. Hardin was compelled to struggle for five years, and the family's straitened circumstances filled the youthful Masters with humiliation—and possibly sowed the seed of class hatred which was such an integral part of his "Populism."

Lee carried coal for the Justice of the Peace and delivered newspapers from door to door. Hardin was ashamed of these activities, and when his income improved, he expressed his disapproval. Since Lee received no allowance, he chose to continue earning his dollar a week.

Hardin detested the prohibition against liquor enforced by the townspeople. He believed in the saloon and said so. He played poker openly, making no effort to conceal the cards when visitors arrived. He made it a point of pride to abstain from church, incurring added enmity by his absence. His refusal to conform proved costly. The religious pillars of the community prevented him from realizing his ambition to become county judge.

Lee was proud of his father's liberalism, and he emulated it throughout his life. He hated the asceticism of Lewistown, which had taken bread out of his family's mouth. He resolved to be a free thinker, free lover, and free drinker. His ideal of the village became a composite of New Salem and a kind of provincial Athens in which there was a democracy with very little government, in which men thought, loved and drank as they pleased, and in which no money powers enslaved the group for the benefit of the few.

Soon after Lee Masters was admitted to the practice of law in 1891, Alfreda, one of his amours, succumbed to a ribbon clerk in her father's store. The defeat overwhelmed Masters. After castigating her choice, he added:

> Her father belonged to the church set which defeated my father for the judgeship. All this filled me with indignation, and I decided to go to Chicago, to get away from village spites, the melancholy of the country, and the bad will that followed me everywhere.

Chicago and Populism

In Chicago Masters was employed for ten months by the Edison Company to collect bills and try cases on their behalf. His salary of fifty dollars a month was inadequate, and he frequently pawned his watch. He lived in boarding houses, where he spent his Sundays and holidays producing verse. Some of it was published under pseudonyms in the Chicago *Inter-Ocean* and in Eugene Field's column, "Sharps and Flats," in the Chicago *Daily News*. Masters' interest in poetry was matched by his interest in politics, and the excitement of the 1892 election stirred him. Already he was alive to the aims of the Populists:

> The Populists in 1892, under the leadership of James B. Weaver of Iowa, declared that the nation was on the verge of moral, political and material ruin as the result of the scheme which had been carried out giving bond-holders the power to issue the money of the country. They therefore denounced the national banks, they demanded an income tax, and postal savings banks, and the national ownership of railroads. They announced the doctrine that the land was the natural heritage of the people and should not be monopolized.

Masters was in sympathy with the Populist spirit. While he voted for Cleveland, the Democratic candidate, he advanced Populist reasons for so doing.

> I voted for Cleveland in 1892 because he promised the country a tariff for revenue only, and because the platform on which he ran was for bimetallism and against the trusts.

Later, Masters decided that Cleveland was a secret and evil friend of the trusts. He became so partisan that he noted Cleveland's demise with satisfaction. He stated: "One wave of the rising agrarian movement which afterwards affronted him as Populism and read him out of the Democratic Party as Bryanism struck him while he was Governor of New York."

Masters disliked his work and shrank from the encounters with insulting bullies and supercilious secretaries from whom he had to collect bills. Collecting money from the poor did not increase his admiration for a city monopoly which was all-powerful. Consequently, in 1893, he opened a law office with a young man slightly older than himself. His associate, with an insight into psychology, insisted that the tripartite name Edgar Lee Masters appear on the door rather than Lee Masters.

Masters was stirred by the abortive march of "Populist" Coxey's army to Washington and by the strike led by Eugene Debs against Pullman in 1894, which was quelled by the use of Federal troops. A statement he made concerning Lindsay might equally have been applied to himself: "It was part of Lindsay's education, a part of the growth of his mind as a poet to live through these years of economic war and tumult."

Concerning the Pullman strike, Masters wrote:

> Government by injunction was just beginning to get hold of American jurisprudence. Instead of considering that the strikers had rights as well as the railroads, Cleveland had no conception of the situation, except that the law should be enforced. Labor may get some rights by arbitration, but never by troops.

The same attitude is revealed when he lamented the defeat of Governor Altgeld in 1896:

> The street railways were happy. Pullman, triumphant in the courts by grace of the Federal administration, was vindicated by the votes of the people. The banks, the Girondists, the Tories of every hue, the clubs of the monopolists sang and danced and rejoiced.

In the emotion-fraught election of 1896, Hardin Masters was chosen as a Democratic delegate from Illinois. He gave his ticket to Edgar Lee, who wrote:

16

Daily I saw the Coliseum, with its thousands of delegates and spectators, seething with wrath against the banks, the tariff, government by injunction, the Supreme Court, plutocracy and Cleveland.

Altgeld, who favored all the Populist measures, was running for re-election as Governor of Illinois. He dominated the Convention until Bryan mounted the stand. Masters wrote glowingly that Bryan

> . . . carried the vast throng into ecstacies of hope. A new day spread its glorious colors before the audience as they heard this young and handsome man declare that the end had come of petitions that were scorned, of prayers which had been mocked, of confidence-enduring poverty in the sod huts of the West which had been betrayed. The people no longer petitioned, they no longer prayed, they no longer asked for relief; they defied the monopolists and the banks. The wild applause that greeted his peroration, the marching of delegates and the tumult of happiness, the rejoicing that Cleveland had been booted from the party, made a scene in all never equalled in an American convention.

Bryan, young, handsome, and eloquent, became the "hero" of the Populists. He was the new Thomas Jefferson; the new Andrew Jackson; and in fact he was closer to the farm voters than either of those leaders.

Bryan voiced the conviction of the Populists that the American economy was based on the farm. In the "Cross-of-Gold" address in the Coliseum he proclaimed:

> The great cities rest upon our broad and fertile prairies. Burn down your cities and leave your farms, and your cities will spring up again as if by magic; but destroy our farms and the grass will grow in the streets of every city in the country.

17

Not everyone was as bewitched by Bryan's oratory and presence. Henry Demarest Lloyd, who had the insight to see that the People's Party would have greater permanence and value as a broadly based reform organization rather than as a pressure group devoted to a few issues, dismissed the free silver movement as a "fake."

> Free silver is the cowbird of the reform movement (he declared). It waited until the nest had been built by the sacrifices and labors of others, and then it laid its eggs in it, pushing out the others which lie smashed on the ground.

Masters, however, worshiped Bryan in 1896. Squire Davis' indifference to Bryan made no impression on him—nor did his Uncle Will's opposition to free silver. He was merely amused when the Chicago *Tribune* dubbed the party which had nominated Bryan "Popocrats" and dismissed his performance as a speech of "forty blatherskite power."

Masters devoted all his energies to his hero's cause by reading books on the money question and persuading the Democratic State Committee to allow him to speak on "free silver" in Petersburg. He appeared at the polling booth in his ward at six o'clock on election morning, relinquishing his vigil twenty-two hours later when the count was completed.

The Bryan tide had ebbed, but Masters remained unaware of it. He clung to the belief that there might yet be a new era, a re-birth of the Republic. Unlike his Irish political henchmen, who were interested in money and offices, Masters was thinking about America's new day and what he could do for it. To this end he organized and became president of the Jefferson Club of Chicago, where the fires of the Democratic Party were to be kept burning, where banquets for Bryan and other celebrities were to be given.

Unlike those Populists who were early disillusioned by Bryan, Masters remained faithful to his idol until 1908. As President of the Jefferson Club, Masters came to know Bryan well; and when Bryan's political ambitions finally made him

aware that his confidence had been misplaced, he reacted
with the bitterness of one personally betrayed. He attacked
Bryan in "The Cocked Hat":

> For we were radicals,
> And he wasn't a radical.
> Eh? Why, a radical stands for freedom
> And for truth.

In a second poem, "The Christian Statesman," he wrote:

> The Christian Statesman having lost his hair
> Betrays the Midas ears—the oily smile
> Beams on the republic he has overthrown!

Elsewhere, having accused Bryan of betraying the liberals,
of pathological opportunism, Masters wrote:

> I saw Bryan at Madison Square Garden in 1924, not
> applauded but hissed; not smiling, young trim, inspiring
> and inspired, but hard, set of mouth, dogmatic, shriveled,
> old and malicious. The defeat of 1896, and his later de-
> feats, had sculptured him to this figure. It had been
> better if he had died, or been assassinated in 1896.

In order to understand Masters' partisanship for a man or
an idea one should contrast his "Bryanism" with his "Altgeld-
ism." John Peter Altgeld was a Populist of stature who never
deserted the cause, and for this reason he remained in Masters'
pantheon. Throughout his life Masters had nothing but praise
for Altgeld. Recalling his first visit to Altgeld's office, he wrote:
"I should like him to know here and now that I am one of his
admirers." Then Masters proceeded to enlighten a later generation:

> He had a genius for organization; and the Republican
> press tried to stop him by calling him a "brazen dema-
> gogue," a "fomenter of Know Nothingness," a "million-

aire labor leader." And this was because he was attacking the convict labor system, police brutality, the inequality of criminal sentences, unnecessary imprisonments, improper arrests, cruel treatment in prison . . . the arbitration of strikes, the right of labor to organize.

Masters concluded his eulogistic article:

> Yet who knows? Old questions have a way of rising again; and it is possible that some day Altgeld will be appealed to as the man who made the great stand against American imperialism and American plutocracy.

Masters had respected Altgeld's courage in pardoning some of the condemned Haymarket anarchists. And when Altgeld was defeated for governor and publicly insulted, Masters lost some of his faith in "the people":

> Altgeld firmly believed that the people . . . whom he trusted with a faith not excelled by Jefferson, would return him to power and show their appreciation of what he had done and tried to do for them. His disappointment was sharpened by the insult that was given him on the occasion of the inaugural of the new governor.

Masters later transferred some of his enthusiasm for Altgeld to Carl Sandburg, who quoted Masters verbatim:

> 'They stripped him [Altgeld] to the bone, drove him into a terrible loneliness, but I don't believe those who say he died of a broken heart. He had hidden strengths. In his fifty-four years he lived a thousand years. It could be that five hundred years from now his name will stand out like that of Cromwell or William of Orange.

In fact John Peter Altgeld was the only political leader to emerge during Masters' long lifetime who inspired Masters' lasting admiration. And the extent to which Masters' feelings

could be aroused, decades later, shows how emotionally involved he was. In 1940, Masters wrote to Theodore Dreiser:

> Altgeld has an obscure grave somewhere near Chicago,
> but where his spirit is I would rather not say. My eyes
> are so clouded with water that I cannot go on.[2]

Masters considered the defeat of Bryan in 1896 as a signal
for a reaction toward plutocracy. He pointed out that of the
318 important industrial trusts existing in 1905, 236 were
formed after 1898. He wrote:

> Statistics show that 1 per cent of the families of the
> United States own 99 per cent of the national wealth.
> And why is this? It is due to the fact that 1 per cent has
> used the taxing power and the bank power to accumulate
> capital to the point of such ownership. It is due to the
> fact that the poor pay two-thirds of the indirect taxes;
> that the banks issue and control, as shown by the statistics
> of 1904, one-fifth of the circulating money of the land;
> and that by the power of the tariff tribute is levied and
> fabulous fortunes concentrated in the hands of its
> favorites.

Here, appropriately in *Tom Watson's Magazine,* Masters is
echoing a basic Populist tenet that money power was destroying the Republic. Indeed, he held this conviction with such
fervor that it amounted to a religion, and he devoted much of
his life to re-exploring American history, which he felt was
written as the monopolists and Christians wanted it written,
with the sole aim of discovering men who resisted money and
class privileges, and finding villains who sought and furthered
them—and much of his literary output amounts to a revision
of history by an agrarian sympathizer.

Chapter III

EDGAR LEE MASTERS

The Historian

From 1892 to 1901 Masters wrote articles and pamphlets on the Constitution and on politics which he published, and poetry which he hid. One reason for his greater confidence in political writing may have been the factor of success—success achieved by iconoclasm, by "nay-saying." Masters attacked Chief Justice Marshall, calling him "a wrecker of the Constitution" via the doctrine of "implied powers." This article attracted attention in Chicago, and raised his name as a protestor against all that was being done by Republicans. He was praised and censured, nationally, in newspapers and in law journals.

This attention was a heady wine for Masters, for he was to include historical reappraisements, whether they belonged or not, in most of his prodigious production of fifty-two volumes of poetry, plays, novels, biographies, and essays; as well as in scores of magazine articles and book reviews. The man who was to correct the "muck of money and falsehood" and the "false American histories," to use his later terminology, was hardly an impartial observer. He was like State's Attorney Fallas of *The Spoon River Anthology*, a "legalist, inexorable and bitter." For Masters always sought to win his case; and to this end he was willing to gather an enormous amount of fact, sometimes trivial and circumstantial, and to distort truth enthusiastically.

If Masters' concept of American history and his evaluation of historical personages is not reliable, it is at least consistently two-dimensional. There are heroes and villains, good and evil, Americanism and un-Americanism, country and city. There are no values in between, no mixtures, no greys. Neither is there any re-evaluation to correspond with growth on the part of Masters. Whatever Masters believed in from his twenty-third to his thirty-seventh year, 1892-1906, the years in which he was exposed to Populist influence, he continued to believe until his death in 1950. Any changes he made in his footnotes to history were due to his having read more material to substantiate his prejudices. For this reason, dates are not important in a study of Masters' mind. Masters never outgrew the Populist agrarian in himself.

Foremost among Masters' heroes was the father of Populism, Thomas Jefferson. As a lawyer, Masters could appreciate the contributions of Jefferson to political science and to American jurisprudence. It was Jefferson's strictures upon the opinions of John Marshall which had safeguarded the Constitution. It was Jefferson's "clairvoyant eye" which had "forecasted the aggressions of the Federal courts" and called them "mines and sappers of the Constitution."

When Theodore Roosevelt, whom Masters considered a humbug and a militarist in "slouch hat and clanking spur," was at the height of his glory Masters found the best way to debunk him: to contrast Thomas Jefferson to him. Masters wrote:

Jefferson's birthday in these days is not generally celebrated at the banquet board. His character lacked the militant element which lends itself to paganistic rites of the feast, the toast, and the high-sounding eulogium. He won no battles, he conquered no visible foes, he captured no concrete strongholds. His life was intellectual and peaceful.

He was devoted to liberty and to trust. There was no humbug in him. He developed no mysticism of a flag with which to enslave the minds of his fellows. . . .

23

Who disputes his philosophy? Who says that all should not be equal before the law? Who says that men do not have the inalienable rights of life and liberty, that the office of government is to secure these and that governments derive their just powers from the consent of the governed?

It was Masters' conviction that "no thoroughgoing life of Jefferson" had been written. Masters had tried to rectify this by mentioning Jefferson often in his works, by writing poems to Jefferson. And in 1933, when Franklin Delano Roosevelt was inaugurated as President, Masters lost no time in writing to him concerning "the lamentable absence of a memorial to Jefferson in Washington." [3]

Opposed to Jefferson was Alexander Hamilton, evil incarnate in Masters' version of American history:

> It was Hamilton born on the Island of
>   Nevis
> In the West Indies, not born in the New
>   World nor in the spirit of it,
> Born out of wedlock to a woman named
>   Leirne
> Who loaded the Old World on the back
>   of the New World
> Who inoculated the New World with the
>   diseases of the Old World. . . .
>   *The New World*

It was Hamilton who planted deep into the body of the Constitution germs of monarchy; it was Hamilton whose ghost stalked through the history of the Republic. His funding scheme, according to Masters, was an artful creation of a permanent public debt designed to enable the plutocracy to draw to itself the wealth of the unsuspecting people. In a word, Hamilton was the man "who took the bread of the poor and gave it to the banks."

Fortunately, the popular revolution under Jefferson pre-

24

vailed and Hamilton is dismissed as "the West Indian wanderer whom Aaron Burr slew at Weehawken." Hamilton's physical death, however, did not kill his ideas. Masters considered him as the progenitor of the Republican Party, a party for which Masters developed an implacable hatred, likening it to a snake coiled round the flag pole of Liberty.

With characteristic finality, Masters made the Democratic Party the champion of "Americanism":

> The Democratic Party serves and expresses Americanism, or it is nothing, and has no excuse for being. The Republican Party betrays Americanism and has always betrayed it. . . . When blue-eyed Billy Sheehan made Judge Parker the candidate in 1904, and the East took control of the party, I yet held my nose and voted for him.

Masters persisted in voting Democratic until 1940, when he voted Republican for the first time, explaining to Dreiser that he voted for Wilkie mainly to get rid of the Roosevelts and their teeth.[4]

Masters' good-and-evil approach to history is amply recorded throughout his writings. In *The New World* (1937), a book-length narrative poem, Masters presented, to cite a *Time* reviewer,

> a detailed catalog of slips whereby the New World has fallen from its original promise of a New Age to the 'age of brass' following Appomattox; to the 'age of gas' initiated by 'logo-lyrist' Woodrow Wilson, finally to the 'age of soap-grease' sponsored by Franklin Roosevelt.

The roster of heroes in this volume are Washington, Jefferson, Jackson, Emerson, Whitman, Lee. In *Poems of the People* (1936) Masters' title clearly indicates the "Populistic" bias that holds the collection together. Here the roll call of "the people's" heroes includes Washington, Jefferson, Daniel Boone, Meriwether Lewis, Andrew Jackson and Martin Van Buren. In *The Tide of Time* (1937), Masters had intended to write a

25

novel dealing with the Civil War period; nevertheless, in 680 "close-type" pages, he managed to range from the War of 1812 down to the depression of 1930.

The dates of publication of the above books indicate that in the 1930's Masters was concerned with American history. He had, however, written on the same material in *The Blood of the Prophets* (1905), a collection of poems which he published under the pseudonym of Dexter Wallace, and in *The New Star Chamber and Other Essays*, (1904), a collection of political articles, some of which were reprinted in *Tom Watson's Magazine*.

Masters never shrank from repetition; he had no qualms about writing the same thing *ad nauseam*, whether he had readers or not. His approach to literature was similar to that of a circus barker or a modern advertising "pitch-man," who recites his "piece." Masters' "piece" was that America had deteriorated.

In *Blood of the Prophets*, Masters published two companion poems: "America in 1804" and "America in 1904." In these two poems rural America and imperialistic America were contrasted. In the same volume appeared "Banner of Men Who Were Free":

> Flag of a noble race, no longer our
> flag in truth,
> Borne by a hostile hand in a cause of shame,
> Give us the banner that flapped in the eyes
> of the nation's youth.
> And sent a thrill through the world of its
> faultless fame.

In prose, Masters paraphrased the same idea thus:

> We are no longer the Maud Muller of nations drinking at the well, ashamed at our calico gowns and sighing for the city far away. We have become great. We have painted our eyebrows and put on our scarlet robes.

Masters' pantheon gives a clue to what he considered the outer limits of America's virtuous period. All the political persons, with the exception of Altgeld and Bryan, are pre-Civil War. The Civil War marked the turning point in American history; it killed America's past; it made way for corruption in government, for monopoly, for imperialism. Lust for money inspired the Civil War; the Civil War was, in Masters' interpretation of history, "of the Jews."

Opposing money, monopoly, imperialism, was the South. Masters conceded that the South was a slavocracy, but he regarded it as less evil than the plutocracy of the North.

> A money power [Masters wrote in one of his historical novels *Children of the Market Place*] is fast growing up in this country which will rule the country so thoroughly that the small dictation of the cotton industry of the South will not be a comparison. Slavocracy is only one of the scales on the tail of the dragon of plutocracy. Gold and silver, tariffs, subsidies, colonies, banks of issue— these are the claws and teeth of the big slavery.

Though Masters imposed the issues of Populism and McKinleyism on the Civil War, he was in one sense consistent. The agrarian South with its plea for "states rights" was closer to the ideals of Jeffersonian democracy and Populism than was the North. The South stood for less government, for more individualism, and, most important, for the romantic past. Masters, quite logically, made the South the champion of liberty and General Lee another of his heroes.

It was Masters' conclusion that the cause of the South was the cause of the Republic. And with characteristic disregard for reality, he suggested that America be divided into two Republics so that in one of them the states could be sovereign.

Masters' insistence on fighting the Civil War, decades after the event, despite the fact he was not a Southerner, despite the fact that he had lived mostly in Chicago and New York City, reveals the depth of his agrarian prejudice. Nor can this prejudice be accounted for by the fact that his forebears had been Southerners, or that Hardin Masters had suffered in Lewistown as a "Copperhead." The "real" reasons for this prejudice, to cite Professor James Harvey Robinson, were most likely concealed from Masters. Squire Masters had taught him that the Civil War had been wicked and unnecessary. But this teaching was hardly enough to create the obsessive hatred Masters developed for Abraham Lincoln.

Lincoln, with Jefferson and Jackson, belonged to the Populist trinity. He was a Kentuckian by birth, a "log-cabin" man, born poor, self-educated, hardy, hard-working, incorruptible, humble, dedicated to "the people." He had all the dimensions of a folk hero, and he had given his life in the cause of freedom. Consequently it is no surprise that the Populists of the '90's were ever ready to invoke his name in the cause of the people.

But to Masters, Lincoln was a villain. In denying the States their sovereignty, Lincoln was not a Jeffersonian, but a Hamiltonian. Like Hamilton, Lincoln had been in favor of more national banks. Lincoln was instrumental in the passing of the Fourteenth Amendment, which protected and perpetuated the corporations and trusts; since they, in their legal suits referred to themselves as "individuals"—and as such they were guaranteed life, liberty and pursuit of happiness. And, worst of all, Lincoln had obstructed the legal secession of the Southern States. In short, Lincoln was not one of the people, nor a champion of the people; rather he was an architect of plutocracy.

To prove his points, Masters undertook *Lincoln, the Man,* an analysis of Lincoln. Masters was determined to show that Lincoln did not belong in the Populist pantheon: that he did not equal Jackson in character, in gifts as a soldier, or as a statesman; and that he was inferior to Jefferson in mind, in interests, in learning, and in statesmanship.

Lincoln, Masters maintained, was a greedy man:

> It is quite clear altogether that as a lawyer Lincoln did not champion the poor and the downtrodden, he was doing his best to make money, and to that end he took

the side of the strong. In this day in Chicago or New York City he would have graduated into corporation practice, as far as he could have done so.

In fact, according to Masters, Lincoln "did more to sabotage the Constitution than even Hamilton and Webster for the forces of empire and privilege"; he handed the country over to the plundering monopolists and the banks.

Such an agent of the plutocrats could hardly have the honesty and strength of character of the people. Masters' characterization and analysis of Lincoln was in keeping with the inhuman stereotypes that "muckraking" Populist writers such as Frank Norris had created of enemies of the people. Lincoln, according to Masters, was a man of contradictions and inconsistencies; a sophist; a hypocrite who was ashamed of his early life and poverty; a lazy man. He was a man of intellectual cunning, a twister of dialectic, an equivocator; he was superstitious, melancholy, mentally unbalanced, cold, undersexed, reticent, deficient in aesthetic gifts.

The assassination of such a monster could only be a service to humanity, and the assassin a hero of the people—accordingly, Masters depicted John Wilkes Booth as a lover of liberty:

> God! If I die, send my mother word
> I died for my country.... Now I mean to do,
> And do alone what armies could not do.
> *Gettysburg, Manila, Acoma*

And Booth's father is made to approve the deed:

> I know, I think
> He knew the dangers, agonies ahead
> For a boy who sets his feet along the path
> To free the world.
> "Richard Booth to His Son"

The fact that Lincoln had freed the slaves was not important to Masters, who was more concerned with the mastership of the Republic by "millionaires." For Masters could see no men to overlord the millionaires, a lack which meant the end of the Republic and the perpetuation of a plutocracy.

Masters' presentation of Lincoln as the wrecker of the Union had repercussions; he was attacked by "poetasters, professors, local Illinois patriots," though an attack from such people was so much grist for Masters' anti-intellectual mill. But Vachel Lindsay was offended; and Carl Sandburg, to whom Masters claimed he had given the idea of a Lincoln biography, grew cool towards him. Masters never relented; to his friend, Dreiser, who was not "literarily" involved with Lincoln, Masters wrote gratuitously:

> This here is Lincoln's birthday and there is the usual chatter about the flat-boat man who made useless war. People will moan about wars that threaten now, but if you show that Lincoln could have prevented war, and didn't do it for political reasons, for reasons connected with patronage and power of a new party, you are set down as an enemy of beauty and truth.[5]

Beauty and truth were to be found in the person of Stephen A. Douglas, the antagonist of Lincoln, whom the "monopolist-paid" historians had slandered by picturing him as "crafty Douglas." Actually Douglas was immensely devoted to America and he wanted to make it great and enlightened. He was a true Jeffersonian in that he held "there is a limit to the legitimate interference of collective opinion with individual independence."

Masters was not saying anything he had not said before; he had previously published a novel, *Children of the Market Place*, which was centered on Stephen A. Douglas' career and which was also intended to convey the era in which Douglas had lived. This work, unlike the Lincoln book, had been a labor of love, prodigious research going into it. "Masters must have," conjectured Harry Hansen, "dug deeply into archives, for the book was freighted with an overwhelming mass of detail." But Masters could well have spared himself the added labor, for

30

he knew what he was going to say and how the book would end. The Douglas theme was only a vehicle for Masters to comment on America from the years 1833 to 1900, to echo his convictions on Andrew Jackson, Webster, Clay, Calhoun, the Mexican War, the Civil War, and Wall Street. And at the end of the novel, the protagonist, old and decayed (like America), observes: "A freight train goes by nearly a mile long. It is laden with coal, oil, iron. I can't believe the soil is free. Coal and oil and iron [sic] have too much of it."

The Biographer and Critic

The Populist bias of Masters, with its idiosyncrasies that set him apart from other literary Populists, can best be seen in his biographies of Mark Twain and Walt Whitman, whose spiritual descendant he was; in his biography of Vachel Lindsay, whose friend and contemporary he was. For Masters' mind seemed to follow a pattern which roughly encompassed the following questions: When and where was the subject born? of what stock? of what economic class? What was his education? his attitude toward money? toward Lincoln? toward the Civil War? toward Wall Street? toward the people? toward rural America? toward urban America?

Masters' biography, *Whitman*, came immediately after *Lincoln, The Man*. The choice of subject was consonant with Masters' temperament and prejudices. Whitman was a democratic equalitarian, a rebel against social restriction, a man who knew what the "real" America was. Masters took pains to quote at length from Whitman's *Specimen Days*:

> I wonder if people of this continental inland must know how much of first class art they have in these prairies—how original and all your own—how much of the influences of a character for your future humanity . . . this favor'd central area of (in round numbers) two thousand miles square seems to be fated to be the home both of what I would call America's distinctive ideas and distinctive realities.

31

Masters was well satisfied with Whitman's ancestry and environment. It was American oak, not tainted with anything foreign: "The Whitmans were distinguished for long life and fecundity. They were a tall vigorous breed. . . . No poet was ever born into an environment better adapted to the nourishment and development of his genius than was Whitman." Masters went on to describe Whitman as having "a literary mind which catches meanings and contents at a glance." And finally Masters asserted that Whitman had achieved cosmic consciousness.

In spite of this praise, Masters, like Whitman, chose to contradict himself when he felt like contradicting himself. One consequence was that Masters found Whitman's mind "slovenly and disorderly"; and the biography which had begun favorably ended as an attack. The reason for this shift in viewpoint was that some of Whitman's attitudes and actions were not in accord with Masters' prejudices. For example, Whitman's veneration of Lincoln annoyed Masters, who found it to be "nebulous and trivial when examined." Whitman's becoming a male nurse on the Union side served to draw Masters' scathing comment that this action was "as irregular and informal as his verse." Even more offensive to Masters was Whitman's acceptance of the Civil War, particularly when Whitman knew the South "was not solely at fault for secession, yet he called secession the foulest crime of the time. He should have known that Lincoln could have prevented the war, yet he worshipped Lincoln."

Masters simply could not understand these lapses on Whitman's part, and he asked rhetorically: "Was Whitman's mind, however, made up about the war? He was a child of Jefferson, of Jefferson's republic and of the Declaration of Independence." Then Masters arrogated to himself the right to declare: "Whitman's heart was not in the war." A mild statement which reveals that Whitman was, in Masters' opinion, to be kept on the side of the angels, on the side of the people.

Mark Twain did not fare as well as Whitman, for Masters' biography was decidedly hostile. Fifteen years before its publication Masters had laid down the dictum that the artist necessarily . . . reacts to the conditions under which he lives; so that the state of the country may have very much to do with poetry. . . . We must follow Whitman's advice to the states: obey little, resist much.

In Masters' opinion, Mark Twain's crime was that he had not resisted at all. On the contrary, he had been blind to what Masters had described in *Whitman* as America's

> . . . foulest period. The South had been crushed and was being devoured by political buzzards. Liberty was dead in the land. A riot of crooked finance had crazed and demobilized the people. The Credit Mobilier sent forth its stink. The banks got what legislation they wanted in order to pick the pockets of the nation. Monopolies began to rise like giant poisonous weeds in the soil enriched by the blood of the youths whom Whitman had nursed.

Mark Twain was born in the holy period, "the last years of Andrew Jackson's powerful [sic] rulership as President." His "best books came out of the frontier, out of the uncontaminated American soil of the West, owing their quality to nothing foreign whatever." According to Masters, works such as *Tom Sawyer*, *Huckleberry Finn*, and *Life on the Mississippi*, came from Twain's heart, from "days magically lived." But, while these works bore "all the marks of the creative imagination . . . much of his later work was the product of the comedian, the buffoon, the protester, the satirist, the sceptic, the embittered soul."

Like Whitman, Twain had failed to realize that the cause of the South was just, an unforgivable sin considering the fact that Twain was a Southerner, "born of slaveholding stock and of Democrats." Worse yet, Twain chose to become a Republican and abolitionist, an apostasy which damned both Twain and most of his literary work not connected with Masters' "Huckleberry-Finnian" dream milieu.

In seeking the cause for this fall from grace, Masters noted that in the fateful year 1861, Twain was twenty-six years of age. Immaturity, therefore, could not be advanced as a mitigating circumstance, even though Masters emphatically contended that Twain was "puerile, and in a large measure he remained puerile to the end of his days." The fatal flaw, Masters agreed with William Dean Howells, lay in the fact that Twain had become "completely de-Southernized," which meant that "Missouri, the West, idyllic scenes of the people of the soil, all that he knew in his youth were oozing out of him."

When one became "de-Southernized" he could only become "Easternized" and tainted with the money-rot. Having to choose between money and the destruction of his genius, Twain chose money. He was cursed with "a spirit which stirs itself to acquire money and distinction, and at worst put back into oblivion the beginnings of the village." Emerson and Whitman, Masters pointed out, had escaped "this form of rot."

Masters also censured Twain for not ridiculing "the grabbers and the capitalists," and complained that "he did nothing and said nothing to make enemies of the ruling powers." Then Masters pointed out that Mark Twain means "safe water," and he made the biting observation that Twain had chosen his pseudonym with "fatal accuracy."

In spite of this multiplicity of sins, Twain was a "son of the frontier," and, as such, there had to be some good in him. Consequently Masters found in Twain some things worthy of commendation: Twain had turned to the Democratic Party under Cleveland; he had cried out against the American seizure of the Philippines, and he had seen that Theodore Roosevelt's doctrine of the strenuous life was humbug. Had Twain not been puerile and had he not been corrupted by the East—in the Masters' canon both of these faults often amount to the same thing—he might have been accorded the adulation that was his due for having created the idyllic America which Masters fervently believed in, albeit Masters had not lived in such an America for the very good reason that it had never existed. Moreover, had Twain not become a tarnished idol, Masters might have discovered that he owed much of his own thinking, much of his literary style, and all of his ideal of the village to Twain. Yet Masters remained curiously unaware of his literary relationship to Mark Twain; or, if he were aware of the fact, he steadfastly refused to acknowledge it.

In dealing with the life of Nicholas Vachel Lindsay, Masters was on familiar ground. He had been born ten years before Lindsay, he had known Lindsay from 1914-1926, and his biography, as the sub-title suggests, was to be an evaluation of America as well as of the poet.

From Masters' point of view, Lindsay had much in his favor. He was born in the Republic which still retained some of its ancient glory, before the immigrant hordes had arrived—when the trusts were young, and the farmers still counted as freemen in a republic. Lindsay also had the advantage of being born of good American stock. Writing of Lindsay's mother, Esther Catherine Frazee, who graduated from Glendale Female College in 1869, Masters said:

> It speaks for his nature to note that she stood perfect in her marks from the beginning to the end of her course. All this is revelatory of that America when remote places of life, remote from the cities and magical places of culture spurred the aspiring young, determined to rise from inferior levels, to use every moment of time and to achieve excellence to the utmost.

In addition, Lindsay was born in the holy-land of Illinois: "He is a plant native to the Lincoln country, more native to it than any other American."

In some respects, Masters' life paralleled Lindsay's and because of this Masters often attributed to Lindsay his own feelings. Masters had an awe of his father, and the same awe is ascribed to Lindsay. Like Masters, Lindsay kept notebooks and journals, read much, went to a small Illinois college (Hiram College), and to Chicago to improve his fortunes, where he had to work at odd jobs to sustain himself. Masters also claimed that Lindsay's political development closely resembled his own:

> Lindsay saw and heard Bryan, who sprang up as a leonine protest against the demonetization of silver,

against the oppressions of monopolies, against banks which had gone into "the governing business" when the government should control both itself and the banks; against "government by injunction," and the use of the Federal army in local disturbances; against the tariff, of course; against everything in short which was robbing the poor man and making the rich man richer.

The defeat of the Populists marked the beginning of America's decline.

Lindsay knew that the defeat of Bryan was a defeat of wheat. Many of his purest songs radiate from economic centers like this. When he wanted to make magical Springfield he had in mind Athens of old. . . .

And in the same vein:

Lindsay was the comic muse of the Negro, of the amorphous and awkward days of 1889, which soon turned to the agrarian revolt, under Bryan. . . . All this was Lindsay's America. It was democracy of youth and happiness, strength, and hope. It was America at play, high hearted, free, and just with all wrongs ended in the name of Jefferson.

Masters regarded Lindsay as an innocent, who had "no power of self-analysis, for there was never any struggle of moment in Lindsay's nature between Hebraism and Hellenism." He also considered Lindsay a mystic:

He saw life with the exuberance of Whitman and nothing less, and with the imagination of Coleridge plus, Joseph Smith, plus Jacob Boehme, and plus Swedenborg.

Lindsay developed cosmic consciousness like Whitman: "He was always the soul seeking beauty and God, caring nothing for mathematics and science."

In spite of this "other worldliness," Masters maintained that Lindsay fought the corruptions of capitalism and empire. "He saw that material property was beating down the hope of youth, something that Altgeld saw and expressed." Lindsay protested all his life long against

> the merchant philosophy that has turned America into the hateful paths of empire, and subdued it to the feet of swine. New Salem is the village destined by the pristine vision of the republic. Lindsay knew this and sang a requiem to the past.

Masters' main thesis was that the new, degenerate America had destroyed Lindsay. Lindsay was one hundred per cent American and he remained faithful to the things he knew and which he had taken in with the milk that nourished him. His fate was "to lose himself or his material or both in a foreign environment." "They did not condemn him to the hemlock, but they doomed him by failing to protest against his doom, by failing to give him help out (of) their useless abundance."

According to Masters, part of Lindsay's tragedy originated in the fact that "he had to live in a land already internationalized by the unassimilated breeds of many lands." It was also partly due to

> the vulgarization of the American mind, resulting from cupidity . . . the 2,000,000 subscriber magazine, proving by its popularity that there are not more than 200,000 enlightened people in the United States.

The third contributory factor in Lindsay's tragedy was that he was a Westerner and not an Easterner:

> Not being Eastern American he made but slight impact upon it. . . . He found that there was no union of spirit and mind in America; and that his own West cared more for the East than it did for the West. . . . They preferred the Arthurian legends to those of Johnny Appleseed and Andrew Jackson.

37

Lindsay, whom Masters regarded as "the most important figure native to Illinois," had to waste his time addressing women's clubs in order to live.

> Instead of the song of the Rachel Jane along the hedges of Kansas, he had the iterant questions and nervous giggling of clubwomen in the Middle West, and everywhere over America. All this until his nerves ran blood.

Masters did not hesitate to declare Lindsay America's finest poet. After listing what he considered to be Lindsay's best poems, Masters wrote: "I take the responsibility of saying that they constitute the most considerable body of imaginative lyricism that any American has produced."

Masters also indicted the New York Jews as partly responsible for Lindsay's destruction. The Jews, in Masters' opinion, were the financial controllers of America and the purveyors of poisoned criticism: "The result is that what New York says upon a book is imposed upon Chicago." [6] And New York criticism, according to Masters, could be countered only by William Marion Reedy, a Middle-Westerner, who unfortunately did not live long enough to prevent "the strangulation" of Lindsay.

The Whitman, Twain, and Lindsay biographies were written in the nineteen-thirties, when an author's social criticism often was a measuring stick of his artistic merit. Thus we see Masters elevating Lindsay above Poe because Lindsay wrote: "Art for life's sake" rather than "Art for art's sake,"—a criticism which was not idiosyncratic at the time, for Vernon Louis Parrington, a Populist-influenced critic, in his monumental *Main Currents in American Thought* had devoted only a page or two to Poe because Poe's esotericism did not fit in with "American democracy."

Such non-objective criticism made Masters seem to be flowing with the mainstream of the Leftist criticism of the '30's. He seemed to be at one with the Marxist "nay-saying" against power and privilege, against the "heart-break house of Capitalism." And even Masters was deceived by the similarity of appearances. To Dreiser, who was pouring out a "Stalinist line,"

Masters wrote: "We are in hell's hole here, and all because we deserted our American dream for Hamiltonism." [7] But Masters was not talking about banks and high finance in the same sense that Dreiser and the Marxists were talking about them. The Marxists were interested in big cities, heavy industry, more government, internationalism, popular fronts; for them the farmers were peasants to be collectivized or liquidated should they obstruct the Revolution. Masters was simply re-iterating his Populist convictions of agrarianism, for the village, for states' rights, for less government, for nationalism.

Chapter IV

EDGAR LEE MASTERS

The Lawyer and the Poet

It was Masters' fate to live on in a "deteriorating" America and his tragedy to be Populist-conditioned without having much in common with the farmers and the village which he championed. Masters was a city man who engaged in the "parasitical" profession of law; he was an intellectual who preached anti-intellectualism, but who wanted to write "pure" poetry; he extolled working with one's hands but he did not work with his and, while he loved "the people," he came to despise the "vile majority." Masters was a "bookish" man who had contempt for book-learning. He had absorbed the oratory of agrarian sympathizers and made the agrarian cause his cause on a non-rational, emotional basis. The final irony was that his literary reputation was established on what seemed to be an attack on the village, and he himself was looked on as a scoffer of "hicks."

In view of these contradictions it is necessary to examine Masters' attitudes toward a few specific ideas and people of the American scene from 1900 to 1950. In addition it is necessary to examine some of Masters' plays and, above all, his main poetic efforts since Masters considered himself to be a poet, and his literary reputation is based on his poetry. Any claim of Populist influence, therefore, which does not include Masters' poetry is bound to be thinly substantiated.

Masters' first volume of poems, *A Book of Verses*, was published in 1898, the year in which he, the hater of organized religion and middle-class morality, married Helen M. Jenkins, a strait-laced, middle-class Presbyterian. A *Book of Verses* contained sixty of the four hundred poems which he had written from his teens to his twenty-ninth year: imitative verses bearing such titles as "A Dream of Italy," "Ode to Autumn," "Invocation to Spring"; with such rhymed quatrains as the following:

> In our rough climes where skies are gray
> O'er lifeless trees in winter's time
> We dreamed of a serener day
> Through books of rhyme.

This amaranthine-asphodel type of poetry which had nothing much to do with either Masters or Chicago was hardly Populist, smacking as it did of decadent England, of the East, of culture. And though this volume may have been the beginning of a "twenty year blundering siege of classical poetry," in Alfred Kreymborg's caustic phraseology, it was "essential" Masters, inasmuch as Masters wanted to compose poems like those of Shakespeare, Keats, Shelley, and Browning. That he failed in doing so was not because he lacked realism, as William Marion Reedy thought, or that the "all-hail-to-thee style" of poetry was intrinsically bad, as Harriet Monroe the militant *vers-librist* contended, but that Masters lacked the poetic gift. Masters attacked poetry with the prosaic regularity of a farmer plowing a field.

Irrespective of inherent worth, *A Book of Verses* did contain two themes that had a bearing on Mid-Western Populism—Illinois and Whitman. Particularly prophetic was the nationalism of his Illinois poem:

> Illinois, an empire is thine of billowy fields of glory
> Here shall our epic thrive hereafter.

Of William McKinley and the Spanish American War Masters took the dim view expected of an isolationist and pacifist Mid-Westerner. His poetic comment on McKinley was:

41

In the first bland days of William McKinley
A man with one idea, and that idea wrong,
The idea of making people rich by taxing them.

The New World

And, in prose, Masters wrote of Henry S. Canfield, a brilliant
short story writer who "despaired of the land under McKinley,
and cut his throat one morning." Consequently, in view of
Masters' attitudes toward the deaths of Hamilton and Lincoln,
it would be safe to assume that he would have commended
McKinley's assassin, Leon Czolgosz. For while Masters was a
pacifist where wars were concerned, he apparently condoned
political assassination of those who, in his estimation, wanted
to change America into a plutocracy and an empire.

Toward the Spanish-American War Masters took the anti-
imperialist viewpoint of the Populists that a war would help
bring prosperity, so one was concocted against Spain. Masters
felt so strongly against the conflict that ensued in the Philippines that he determined to speak out against it by writing
Maximilian, a five act drama in poetry and prose. He began
his play at an appropriate point, the Götterdämmerung of
Maximilian, who, though seemingly a despot, is at heart a
Jeffersonian. Napoleon III, having finished with his political
pawn, had withdrawn his support and his soldiers. The American Civil War having ended, the United States could enforce
its Monroe Doctrine against the Austrian usurper. The Republican forces of Juarez close in on the tragic hero, while his
military supporters, household and retainers act as a tragic
chorus.

Escobedo, a general in the service of the Republic, speaks
for Masters:

... we endured privation in the hills
Nursing the life of trampled liberty
Which now defies the despot and the liar
And all who use the word imperialism
To mask the face of greed.

In *Maximilian* Masters voiced the sentiments of the Liberal who will not love his country when it is tainted with "foreign" imperialism. He has Archbishop Labastida, a friend of the French intervention, say:

> I hate them, Excellency—
> Their [America's] foul hypocrisy caught from the British
> Is more than skin deep now. 'Tis in the flesh.

Masters also spoke out at length against the Spanish-American War in *Blood of the Prophets* and *The New Star Chamber and Other Essays*, which we have mentioned. For there was one thing that Masters was clear on and that was that America needed no expansion, no "manifest destiny." In one of his novels, *The Tide of Time*, he was to write:

> Once there were patriots who wanted to take Canada; but whatever that acquisition might have brought us materially it would have thrown the shape out of balance, just as Alaska does. We have to shut our eyes to Alaska. It does not spiritually belong to us; neither do the Philippine Islands. The taking of Mexico would have added a tail to the country, trailing off towards the tropics where we cannot as men of the first stocks have any real interest.

In fact, as we have stated, Masters' opinion was that America was already too large in that it included the non-"states rights" East.

One immediate effect of the assassination of McKinley was the weakening of Jeffersonian democracy, which had been promulgated on the Enlightenment's tolerance of individual heresy. A law was passed to exclude from entry into the United States all who held anarchist beliefs, whether philosophical or not. Under the provisions of this law the Government proposed to deport John Turner, an English philosophical anarchist.

The Free Speech League of New York retained the legal

43

firm of which Masters was a member to manage Turner's case, and Masters took it up with great zeal. He recalled:

> The term 'anarchy' even 'philosophical anarchy' did not reverberate pleasantly in that room where once Webster had cried for 'liberty and union.' I was greatly heckled by the members of the court, and asked to define philosophical anarchy by Judge Harlan.

In 1903, Masters joined Clarence Darrow, who took over Altgeld's law firm. Darrow had much in common with Masters. He had contributed to *Tom Watson's Magazine* pieces which were a curious mixture of fact and fiction, but thoroughly Populist. In one of these entitled "The Doctrine of Assumed Risk," Tony Salvador, an Italian immigrant, loses his leg while working as a railroad switchman. Salvador sues the railroad, but the judge tells the jury that "if Salvador did not know better than to work in such a dangerous place he assumed the risk and they must return a verdict for the defendant, which, of course, they did." In like strain, Darrow's "For the Public Good" tells of Jane Lewis, a sixty-year-old woman who had saved for forty years to buy a home. A railroad, seeking her property, attempted to force her to sell. In her efforts to save her property, Jane Lewis invokes the law, only to find when the case is ended that she has neither property nor money. This story Darrow paralleled with his ironically titled "The Triumph of Justice." In this, a farmer is involved in litigation concerning a piece of land. The case drags on for fifteen years, having such an effect on the farmer's health that he dies.

These three pieces of Darrow's were to reappear in Masters' and Sandburg's writings—and, curiously enough, the situation of helpless, honest folk who were cheated of their savings occurred in Masters' legal experience. In a long suit, Masters defended the Receks, an old hard-working couple of Polish extraction, against the loss of their savings to Jewish real estate sharks. Masters also stubbornly fought a railroad case for several years only to be deprived of part of his fee by a mortgage banker!

During his association with Darrow, Masters wrote five plays (1903 to 1911) to make money, for while he recognized that money had brought decadence to the Republic, he had no fear of being corrupted with the "money-rot." On the contrary, if he were able to amass a small fortune as a playwright, he reasoned, he could abandon his law practice which he hated.

In his first plays Masters restrained himself from expounding political ideas, but the plays were successful only in that they found a publisher, The Rooks Press of Chicago. In the fourth play, *The Locket* (1910), Masters included the feminist plank of the People's Party:

> Eileen: You preach political freedom, democracy and all sorts of good and honest things. Yet government is the corruptest thing in the world; and you makers of history stultify and deny yourselves all the time. You have the ballot, and yet you vote not only to enslave yourselves, but us, the poor women, too, who can't vote.

The above speech is a touchstone of Masters' utter lack of dramatic ability; both language and content are inappropriate for the feminine character, Eileen. The speech is appropriate to Masters, the pleader for a special cause, and to Masters, the projector of Masters.

In the fifth play, *The Bread of Idleness* (1911), Masters reverted to his true form. Drama was forgotten and literary Populism was given full rein. The play deals with a useless idle class which despises itself, a fiction very palatable to the hard-working and the poor. Gertrude, the heroine, says,

> I wish I knew what labor is. I wish I knew hunger. My muscles are flabby—nature is covered over with delicate and useless fat . . . I am sick of this idleness, this vanity, this idiotic pretence.

Tom Herbert, Gertrude's beloved husband, quite agrees with her, and he replies with a speech similar to the essays found in *The New Star Chamber and Other Essays*:

45

America needs a new kind of woman. America needs you. America! I see her! She looks to me like Pallas Athene trying to be herself—flying from the enervating touch of the idle rich, catching up her robes from the outstretched hands of the Philistine, the Pharisee; fighting off those who would remake her in the likeness of Europe with class distinctions and their hatred.

In a situation comparable to Darrow's Tony Salvador, Masters paused, *en passant,* in this play to attack heartless capitalism. Jerrems, a capitalist, refuses to pay an indemnity to a boy who has lost his arm working for him. The boy's co-workers strike, but Jerrems, with capitalist obstinacy, refuses to yield. When, finally, Jerrems is forced to do justice to the boy, he is asked, "In the first place, why didn't you pay the boy for his arm instead of knocking the law?" To which Jerrems replies: "Think of the millions involved." Which is answered by "Think of the arms involved."

Lest his audience or future reader not understand how employers are protected by law, Masters has Ruth, a female labor organizer, speak out to the villain, Jerrems:

> That means you refuse to install safe machinery for these girls to work with. You simply rely on the law that you don't have to have the latest devices in machinery for your factory. . . . How can you have the face to accuse men of violence and lawlessness and conspiracy when you resort to legal fraud and incorporate yourself under the laws of New Jersey so that you can call yourself a citizen of New Jersey and bring your injunction case before that infamous federal judge who sends men to jail for what you call conspiracy—conspiracy! When you yourself are in a trust—in a conspiracy to stifle competition.

The Bread of Idleness has Masters' Populist message, which is, let grass grow in the streets of your cities, a la Bryan, abandon your luxuries, and go back to Nature. Tom Herbert, the protagonist, goes bankrupt, but financial failure is not the beginning of the end as in the success myth of Horatio Alger —or as with Dreiser's Hurstwood. Rather failure is a virtue, the beginning of a new, simple "good" life. Gertrude joins her husband, and she is likewise made happy by their newly acquired poverty. She says, with self-satisfaction: "Our country needs men with the iron of revolutionary heroes. . . . And women like women of the Revolution."

This play is the core of Edgar Lee Masters' Populist literary message. Money and cities bring decadence, corruption, and the death of the Republic. Conversely, nature, the woods, poverty and hard work ennoble the individual and make for the true democracy of the Revolutionary days. The message is a rationalization of the agrarian way of life which usually meant hard work and little more than subsistence. It is a backward-looking message, comparable to Ghandi's wanting to return totally to manufacture by hand; it is also a message of anarchy, born of Rousseau, Jefferson, and Thoreau. For the Populist paradox, which Masters understood intuitively, was that while Populism sought more governmental protection for the people, it was opposed to government, opposed to a complex society which limited or exploited the individual.

With this message which flaunted the success psychology and dollar worship of the East, Masters was in no danger of arousing controversy, for though he published something yearly he attracted no attention. At the age of forty-four, to quote Harriet Monroe, he was "a failure." He had published eleven volumes of poetry, plays, and essays, none of them distinguished, and all of them published by obscure Chicago presses.

Whether Masters had submitted his efforts to Eastern publishers or whether his antagonism to the East had precluded his attempting to do so is a moot point. But Masters' moment came with the publication of a series of free verse epitaphs in *Reedy's Mirror*. These verses attracted considerable attention, and the mighty house of Macmillan became sufficiently interested to publish them in 1915 as a collection entitled, *The Spoon River Anthology*.

Macmillan had put Masters on their list at a propitious moment. *The Spoon River Anthology* became a "best seller," and it earned more money than any previous volume of American poetry. It was to appear in fifty-five editions and at least five languages.

The success story was circulated that William Marion Reedy had become exasperated by Masters' "innocuous" verses, and he had suggested that Masters read the Greek Anthology for its "realism," particularly since realism was in the air. Dreiser's *Jennie Gerhardt* and *The Titan* had appeared; Lindsay and Sandburg were "disturbing everywhere the critical standards." Masters did so, with the result that the first of two hundred and forty-four epitaphs, "The Unknown," was published in the May 29, 1914 issue of *Reedy's Mirror*.

Carl Sandburg has been quoted by Harry Hansen regarding the composition of these poems:

> I saw Masters write this book. He wrote it in snatched moments between fighting injunctions against a waitresses' union striving for the right to picket and to gain one day's rest a week, battling from court to court for compensation to a railroad engineer rendered a loathsome cripple by the defective machinery of a locomotive, having his life round affairs as intense as those he writes of.

Masters has written a thorough account, "The Genesis of Spoon River," of the creation of *Spoon River Anthology*. The names of his characters he drew from the Spoon River and the Sangamon River neighborhoods by combining first names and surnames to suit his purposes. Some names he took from the constitutions and State papers of Illinois. These characters symbolized the world as Masters saw it:

> I came to the conclusion that the city banker was no other than the country banker, the city lawyer the same as the country lawyer, the city preacher the same as the country preacher, and the theology, finance, jurisprudence, society, and the antithesis of good and evil the same in

both city and country town. The village of Lewistown has furnished me a key which unlocked the secrets of the world at large.

Among the individual portraits of *Spoon River* is that of Editor Whedon, who denounced "Populist" Altgeld as the candidate of gamblers and anarchists. Masters buried him close by the river, "where the sewage flows from the village, and empty cans and garbage are dumped, and abortions are hidden." A contrast to Whedon is Carl Hamblin, whose Spoon River *Clarion* was wrecked, and who was tarred and feathered because he published on the day the Anarchists were hanged in Chicago, "I saw a beautiful lady (Justice) with bandaged eyes."

There is Ralph Rhodes who wrecked his father's bank by borrowing money to dabble in wheat. Reminiscent of Bryan is Hiram Scates, who began as a political idealist but sold out, "And out in the cold stood all my followers: Young idealists, broken warriors." There is Adam Wierauch, who fought for Altgeld, but later sold his vote on Charles T. Yerke's street-car franchise. Ironically, big business (Armour) destroys his slaughter-house and butcher-shop enterprise. There is John M. Church, the corporation lawyer, who "pulled the wires with judge and jury, and the upper courts, to beat the claims of the crippled, the widow and orphans, and made a fortune thereat." Masters has rats devour his heart and a snake make its nest in his skull. There is the "Circuit Judge," who has sold justice to the moneyed powers. He is fated to realize that even Hod Putt, the murderer, hanged by his sentence, was "innocent in soul compared with me." The Sunday school superintendent, Henry Phipps, is "the dummy president of the wagon works and the canning factory, acting for Thomas Rhodes and the banking clique." Judge Somers is made by Masters to lie forgotten and unmarked, while Chase Henry, the town drunkard, has a marble block topped by an urn erected to his memory. There is Oats Tutts, whose mother favored women's rights, whose father was the rich miller at London Mills.

The powers of the community—the lawyers, editors, bankers,

mill owners and school superintendent—are depicted by Masters as almost uniformly evil. Nevertheless, there are men of position and wealth, such as John Hancock Otis, who are bonafide democrats, while a laborer like Anthony Findlay, born in a shanty, proves to be a despot:

> And I say to you, Spoon River,
> And to you, O republic,
> Beware of a man who rises to power
> From one suspender.
>
> "John Hancock Otis"

Masters' acid commentaries made it seem as though he were attacking "sterile village life," village life "indigenous to Mid-Western soil." Spoon River was seen by Harry Hansen as "a composite community drawn from his (Masters') knowledge of the little towns along the Sangamon River." One critic complained: "As realism the book obviously will not stand"; while another said, "No one can believe that Spoon River had such an astounding proportion of unfortunates."

Actually the work was not the "revolt from the village" which commentator after commentator found it to be. The latter part of the book is idealistic, as Babette Deutsch has pointed out, celebrating "American idealism as the young Masters had learned it. . . ." Marguerite Wilkinson, noting this quality, has written:

> At least twenty-five of these neighbors . . . must have lived happy lives, full of hearty labor, honest affections, intellectual growth and spiritual aspiration. . . . 'Lucinda Matlock,' Masters' pioneer grandmother, is one such figure. 'Lydia Humphrey' is a little gray spinster for whom the village church is 'the vision, vision of the poets democratized.'

William Marion Reedy had stressed the political aspects of the Spoon River poems even before Masters published them as a book: "Spoon River is somewhat provincial yes, but out of it came Lincoln and the democratic movement, from Greenbackism to the New Freedom." Masters was not indicting the American small town, nor was he criticizing Spoon River's rusticity, rather he was lamenting the corruption of the village, well summarized by Herbert Ellsworth Childs' "Agrarianism and Sex":

> . . . We must remember that Spoon River is rural Illinois in the closing years of the last century. As such, it had already been befouled by the selfishness and vices of a capitalistic society. On a foundation of agrarian good feeling had been laid a smothering superstructure of Business. The village was controlled by the canning works and the banks, which had as willing servants the courts of justice, the press, the pulpit, and public opinion. It was the selfish destruction of liberty that brought so many Spoon riverites to regretful graves. Spoon River represents to Mr. Masters a failure in social justice.

Masters' own comment was,

> I may say that if I had my conscious purpose in writing it and The New Spoon River it was to awaken the American vision, that love of liberty which the best men of the Republic strove to win for us, and to bequeath to time.

If Masters had been lamenting the corruption of the village in his Spoon River poems it is pertinent to examine his attitude toward "the city." He had spent all his adult life, almost a quarter of a century, in the city of Chicago before he had written Spoon River. Temperamentally, he was unsuited for village life, and he had fled Lewistown on reaching maturity. He did return to Petersburg, but only for visits and vacations. Nevertheless, with the exception of Chicago, Masters actively disliked cities. In his works his attitude is frequently as biased as is Wordsworth's in Michael. Everywhere Masters was explicit in his detestation of the city. In one poem he wrote:

You then shall have swine cities with the
     failure
Of the spirit of such a people.
                    "Give Us Back Our Country"

In another poem he equated cities with decadence. To Masters, cities were ugly, nor did he care for their canals, factories, and telephones. Progress was meaningless when "poverty and slaughter starve and take life and thwart the heart's desire." Largeness and growth of population spelled degeneration for Masters:

On State Street throngs crowd and push,
Wriggle and writhe like maggots,
Their noses are flat,
Their faces are broad,
Their heads are like gourds,
Their eyes are dull,
Their mouths are open—
The Great Race is passing.
                    "The Great Race Passes"

And if degeneration were true of Chicago it was even truer of New York City with its Wall Street, its "literary Tammany," its Jews, and its polyglot population. In sum, New York was the antithesis of Masters' "pristine Republic."

Toward Chicago, Masters had an ambivalent attitude. He could hate it and think it ugly because it was a city. Conversely, he could champion it against New York City, and against the world, because it was situated in the holy ground of the agricultural West:

And if it come to pass that Chicago lifts itself to be the richest and most powerful city of the world . . . it will be due to the inner properties of the air which blows about the city from the far west, from the prairies. This makes Chicago a creature of Demeter, the goddess of agriculture, of the laws and civilization.

52

Concurrently with Masters' *Spoon River Anthology* Europe became embroiled in one of its periodic wars, this time a war of unprecedented immensity. In Masters' opinion, World War I was another imperialist war: "Money wants war, and war must have for friend Money." Even more reprehensible was the fact that Mars had "descended from Olympus" and was "policing our national life." The whole atmosphere was alien to the spirit of American democracy. People, he protested, were

> tapped on the shoulder and taken into custody. They had said nothing tremendous. They had only made observations to the effect that they did not like France, or perhaps that Germany had been placed in a situation where it was obliged to act quickly. Life in Chicago became a purgatory. The old happiness was all gone.

Convinced that the war was undemocratic and that it had been imposed upon the people, Masters bitingly pointed out that a "traitor" was one who denounced capital, and who exhorted the crowd to strive for something better than being treated as cannon fodder. He disliked Woodrow Wilson because he had diverted "the economic rising which took place some years before he appeared on the scene," and because of his appointments "which turned out to be tragic consequences for America." [8]

The incidence of war did not divert Masters from striving to achieve what he regarded as desirable social ends. He fought vigorously for the rights of a waitresses' union for a ten-hour day and a six-day week. He wrote an appreciative letter to the *New Republic* (1915):

> Your editorial in this issue of June fifth regarding the defeat of the women's nine-hour bill and the child-labor bill in the Illinois Legislature is very gratifying to the citizens of Illinois, largely in the minority, who hoped to see those bills enacted into laws.

53

At the same time Masters' literary labors increased, for he was now assured of an audience. Always productive, he became prolific, producing five volumes of poetry in as many years. The poetry was typical "uneven Masters," for he seemed to think that poetry was simply an arrangement of lines on a page, which rhymed or did not rhyme. Metaphor, economy, word-music, the labor of the file, insight, lofty thought—these commonplaces of poetry escaped Masters. His poetry was prosaic, while the prose of a contemporary like Sherwood Anderson was poetic.

In these volumes of poetry Masters repeated himself. "Grant and Logan and our Tears," was a Mastersian lament on the failure of America and a exhortation to rouse herself. "Draw the Sword, O Republic," was a similar exhortation; as were "The Typical American," "Come Republic," "The Radical's Message." His "Johnny Appleseed" was a poetic emphasis on the type of man produced by "the pristine Republic." There were no new themes, not even new accentuations. This fact, coupled with the dogmatism inherent in the poems, caused Louis Untermeyer to say: "I have a queer notion that 'Toward the Gulf' is Masters' last volume of poetry; that he has said all he has to say in this medium."

Far from being "written out," Masters was working on "a census spiritual taken of America." *Domesday Book*, modeled on Browning's *The Ring and the Book*, was a supreme effort on Masters' part to equal or surpass his *Anthology*. In twelve thousand lines Masters aimed to bring up to date the history of America, personified by Elenor Murray, who is found murdered near Starved Rock in Illinois:

> This Elenor Murray was America;
> Corrupt, deceived, deceiving, self-deceived.
> Half-disciplined, half-lettered, crude and smart,
> Enslaved yet wanting freedom, brave and coarse,
> Cowardly, shabby, hypocritical,
> Generous, loving, noble, full of prayer,
> Scorning, embracing rituals, recreant
> To Christ so much professed; adventuresome;

Curious, mediocre, venal, hungry
For money, place, experience, restless, no
Respose, restraint; before the world made up
To act and sport ideals, go abroad
To bring the world its freedom, having choked
Freedom at home.

The coroner sets out to find the material evidence from the man who finds the body and the doctor who performs the autopsy and the spiritual evidence from men who had known Elenor or her parents before her. In this way the history of Elenor, her background, her experiences, her dreams are recounted by Masters from many different viewpoints.

In *Domesday Book* Masters' preoccupations with the Republic ruined by mobocracy, capitalism, and alien Judaism have full expression. He struck a new and significant note, however, in his abandonment of the Populist's faith in the demos, giving expression to strong anti-democratic sentiments: "Barrett Bays" gives voice to this new theme:

> The souls,
> Who hated freedom on the sea or earth,
> Had, as the vile majority, set up
> Intolerable tyrannies in America—
> America that launched herself without
> A god or faith, but in the name of man
> And for humanity, so long accursed
> By gods and priests—the vile majority!

In the year he published *Domesday Book*, 1920, Masters was able to retire permanently from his legal practice. He now had adequate leisure for travel and for his literary efforts. Among his many literary labors were sequels to *The Spoon River Anthology* and *Domesday Book*, which added documentation to the evils which had befallen the Republic in three decades since 1896.

Fresh names, foreign and foreboding, appear in the *New Spoon River* (1924): Roland Aborowicz, Euripides Alexopoulos, Gabriel Buissono, Socrates Chrysoverges, Oscar Felleneau, Ernest Fedasko. The poem, "McDowell Young," voices Masters' sentiments concerning this foreign invasion. "Olaf Lindbloom" is representative of the first generation of descendants of the immigrants to Spoon River. Corrupt and venal, Olaf Lindbloom is editor of a Spoon River newspaper, and he publishes, "Girondist doctrines of the largest acceptance thereby increasing my circulation." On the basis of his swollen circulation, he sells advertising space.

The *New Spoon River* is so obviously different from its predecessor that its message did not escape the critics. Harry Hansen wrote:

> Masters endeavors to interpret the lives of those who have died since Spoon River became a standardized community —in other words suffering from the ailments which beset the republic itself—foreign influences, materialism, the madness for money, the lack of high ideals, Spoon River has been 'metropolized'. . . .

The Fate of the Jury, the sequel to *Domesday Book* did not appear until nine years later, Masters' pen during most of the interim being devoted to fiction, some of which will be discussed next, and to his *Selected Poems*, published by the Macmillan Co., in 1925. In *The Fate of the Jury*, Masters voiced his ambivalent attitude toward America. In *Domesday Book* Elenor had participated in World War I "to honor America, this land of promise, of fulfillment, too, which proves to all the world that men and women are born alike of God." This is restated in *Fate of the Jury*:

> Or there's America, so materialistic,
> So heedless, vulgar, cruel, selfish,
> savage;
> But seen another way with her inventions
> Philanthropies, and comforts, beauty too,
> Seems half-divine and climbing to the light.

The juryman, David Borrow, symbolizes the corruption usually accomplished by money, the corruption which defers America's great day indefinitely:

> The corporation noted me. . . . Being hired
> I left the people's cause, and used my
> tongue
> And outward seeming of democracy
> To save the corporation from rabble mulcts
> While making needful money for myself.

David Borrow had sold out to one of the first destroyers of the Union, the railroad corporation.

In *Fate of the Jury* America is accused of being "a vast mediocrity of Materialism," and she is accused of leaving the artist to poverty. And in view of Masters having been a prophet crying in the wilderness, he finally wrote of a theme which had always tormented him. He asked himself whether Idealism was not, after all, merely foolishness. He had meditated frequently upon his participation in politics, particularly concerning his ardor during the "Populist" period, and now he seriously questioned the wisdom of his enthusiasm for politics.

Nevertheless Masters was an incorrigible "nay-sayer," and in 1930, he published *Lichee Nuts*. Here he used Oliver Goldsmith's device of having a Chinese comment upon an Anglo-Saxon civilization, a device which Masters used to belittle America, foreign breeds, and the Republican Party. In the poem, "America Little Boy Yet," Masters stated that what America needed was to suffer the humiliation of losing a war. In "Tammany and Trusts," the Republicans and trusts were depicted as a big thief and the Democrats and Tammany as a little thief. Most interesting of all was the poem "Working Man and Picture," in which Masters equated good with work and sweat, and evil with idleness. Here foreigners were commended because, unlike the contemporary American generation which had declined in moral worth, at least they worked:

All over New York
Strong men at work: Big men, niggers
and whites driving trucks;
Italians digging subways, laying tracks;
Irishmen running long trains,
Putting up sky-scrapers, hammering plates
on ocean liners.
Greeks, Lithuanians, all strong arms,
Lifting rocks, working scoops. . . .
This I call wonderful picture for the
artist.
But Englishman sending cable;
Or Jew counting money;
Or American standing in pulpit. . . .
Nor man wearing spats, dancing with ladies,
Or drinking tea
Not much picture.

Masters continued writing poetry for fifteen more years. His numerous output made it virtually impossible for critics and readers to keep pace with him. In reviewing *Poems of the People*, John Gould Fletcher confessed he "had not been able to keep abreast of Mr. Masters' output," and so had to disclaim knowledge of many works which had places of their own in the canon.

Many of these later volumes we have quoted from to establish the consistency with which Masters reflected Populist influence. And titles such as *Poems of the People* and *More People* leave little doubt about Masters' faith in the people and in America. For though Masters was pessimistic by nature he never gave in to hopeless despair. His continual scolding was meant as a corrective since he had very definite ideas as to what the Republic might have been had it not been diverted from its natural, agrarian course. We have mentioned these ideas throughout the preceding pages. Now we shall examine them as they appeared in Masters' novels and later poetry.

The Novelist

Master's first novel, *Mitch Miller,* was inspired by an enthusiastic conversation he had had with a sister of Theodore Roosevelt concerning *Tom Sawyer* and *Huckleberry Finn*. *Mitch Miller* echoes both of these books—with the difference that Mitch is an idealization of Masters as a boy. Mitch moves to Petersburg, where he hunts for buried treasure and tries to duplicate Tom Sawyer's exploits. Mitch is a dreamer and a poet; he is representative of the sweet type of youth "the prairie could have developed if it had been let alone."

In this novel of boys and a boy's town Masters, the mordant castigator, had a subject which was dear to his heart. One consequence was that his language became quiet and unobstructive, his tone sentimental. But Masters was faced with the problem of what to do with Mitch, who would have to grow up in America, in which Masters himself had been thwarted:

> I feel that no poet in English or American history ever had a harder time than mine was in the beginning in Lewistown, or among a people whose flesh and whose vibrations were better calculated to poison, to pervert, and even to kill a sensitive nature.

Masters' solution was to kill Mitch off. Skeeters Kirby, Mitch's best friend, reflecting on Mitch's death, incurred in the boyish activity of stealing a ride on the railroad, reflects in an epilogue, thirty years after the event, that it was just as well that Mitch had not lived to see America "gone to the dogs."

To a critic unfamiliar with Masters' themes the epilogue seems a curious destruction of his whole mood of nostalgia and sentimentality, but Masters with unfailing consistency had planted his Populistic pessimism in the novel: there is a sermon on hating the dollar and gold; there is an insistence that the good American "stock" has been killed in the Civil War, that new strange breeds of foreigners are destroying the Republic.

Masters' final pronouncement is that the Republic has been throttled by gold and that the old liberties have perished.

Masters' fictional autobiography was too interesting a subject to abandon with the death of Mitch Miller. The sequel, *Skeeters Kirby*, is even more autobiographical than its predecessor. Parallels with Masters' life are found in Skeeters' studying law against his own inclinations to please his father; in his series of love affairs and unfortunate marriage; in Skeeters' seeing himself as "an idealist in a materialistic world doomed to continual defeat and betrayal."

Mirage completed the Mitch Miller trilogy. Opening with Skeeters Kirby at the age of thirty-three, it leaves him at the age of forty-one still confused and muddled, his life still a mirage.

In this novel, money not only corrupts the Republic but the natural hungers of the heart. Becky Norris, instead of marrying Skeeters Kirby, marries a rich and aging man. Tom Megary, a detective, says: ". . . money that's a big thing by itself. For either in marriage or in the love game it's money." Skeeters Kirby shows signs of changing his mind about money, and begins to doubt his literary endeavors which have "disturbed his earning money as a lawyer and given him only an impossible dream." American materialism, which destroys the lover, also destroys the artist, because

> chances are so great for material success that not to take them excites the opposition of the community. Poverty is harder to bear because it is considered so unnecessary and evokes no sympathy. And the artist himself feels all this and undergoes a failure of faith in himself, and he loses concentration. He grows to feel ashamed.

Becky Norris echoes the feminist ideas voiced by Gertrude of The Bread of Idleness: "Women are not going to be bought and sold any more. They're going to vote and win things." Nevertheless, she has sold herself, and, instead of happiness, attains only increased neurosis. Masters, speaking as Skeeters, gives her the same antidote he had given Gertrude:

You are not neurotic. You had a wonderful girlhood of open air life and work; and you are really as strong as a woman can be. But this life! Why it will kill anyone. You don't get air, you don't get exercise, and you naturally brood and waste in this environment.

En passant, Skeeters Kirby voices the anti-war sentiments of Masters as regards World War I; he advocates "repaganization" as a means to save China and America. He tries to define what a republic is, concluding: "It's the hearts of the people"; and he points out that one day America will see that "Alexander Stephens was prophetical when he said that the cause of the South was the cause of the Republic."

Thus what had begun as a boy's story ended with Masters writing an autobiography, which he rewrote later as *Across Spoon River; An Autobiography*.

Kit O'Brien likewise grew out of *Mitch Miller*. Mitch's death at the hands of a railroad brakeman is repeated. The novel depicts the conflict of a small town with railroad interests, and through Kit O'Brien mirrors the small town, the river world and its people. O'Brien, like Jack Kelso, is a wanderer, going from experience to experience, oppressed by injustice.

While Masters admits that *Kit O'Brien* is part of the canvas of the small town, he is at pains to defend his native Petersburg:

> Wherever there is expressed here any criticism of the characters placed upon the stage of Petersburg, or upon the civilization portrayed as belonging to it, I ask the reader to shift his imagination to the American small town in general, and not to Petersburg in literalness. I love that town of my boyhood, its people and its ways too deeply to displease them, or to say anything but good of them (Preface).

Nuptial Flight was a variation on a familiar theme, namely that pioneers and country life bring health and happiness, while cities bring decadence. This novel begins as a farm idyll

61

of the 1840's and 1850's. Grandfather William Houghton, and his congenial wife, Nancy, work hard and prosper and give a wholesome beginning to their five children. Their son Walter Scott Houghton mates wrongly and lives a life of frustration. All three of his children—Alfred, the musical genius, the beautiful Elaine, and young Bertram, the shrewdest of the three— are, like their father, destined to suffer frustration. Their one hope of growing whole again is to return to the protection and society of their grandparents.

In 1937, fully ten years after *Kit O'Brien*, appeared *The Tide of Time*, Masters' last novel. Faithful to the pattern of its predecessors, the setting is a small Illinois town; it depicts the lives of small town people; contains a running commentary on American history, and a lament on the loss of old freedoms and old happiness:

> We have the damnedest situation here you ever saw. This town was once a wonder for friendliness and goodwill, and yes, by God, for liberty. Now it's growing bigger and bigger and richer all the time, and meaner every minute.

William Jennings Bryan visits Ferrisburg. In the election of 1896, the protagonist, Leonard Westerfield, runs as the People's Party's candidate. The excitement of the Chicago Convention of that year is recounted.

> By April 6, 1896, great insurrection existed in Cuba, but it was not noticed in Ferrisburg where the public mind was concerned with the future action of the Democratic Party: would it declare for free silver, or would the bankers control the convention, as they had always done since the days of Jackson?

But the country, agrarian America, lost out to the city. "Money and monopoly had given the city this exhausting advantage over the country." At Eighty-three, Leonard Westerfield had seen the country change into a plutocracy which was rapidly becoming a dictatorship:

Well, I've seen a good many panics. But this panic now in the year 1930 is a seismic sinking. The whole economic and governmental structure is shaking to its fall. And since prohibition has swept away the whole Bill of Rights, and plutocracy has changed the laws you will see this growing despotism produce a practical dictatorship. The plutocracy during the years of my life has devoured the people.

Unexpectedly, the book ends on a final triumphant note, a *non sequitur* to all that has gone before:

After everything has been said, after every complaint has been made, America is a better country and life in it is better than when Leonard Westerfield was born.

The evidence that Masters was more interested in proving a thesis than in the novel as an art form is conclusive. Nothing was lost to the novel, for Masters lacked the novelistic gift as much as he lacked the poetic gift. The best of his efforts was the first, *Mitch Miller*, but like any other imitation it could not compete against the Twain originals. In addition the "roaring twenties," the "Jazz Age" was little interested in Masters' nostalgia, in his pristine America. The genteel decadence of F. Scott Fitzgerald was far timelier than sweet agrarianism, and the realism of Dreiser's *American Tragedy* more prophetic of the pessimism and "cult of violence" that was to come.

What is of interest is the triumph of age, Masters' mellowing, i.e., his admission that America was a better country and life in it better than it had been during the years preceding the Civil War. But for Masters it was too late to change his themes; he could live only in the past and plead for his old gods.

Conclusion

In 1928, Amy Lowell had noticed that it seemed "as though some obscure instinct of relation set his (Masters') mind echo-

63

ing with old times, old words, old pictures." Miss Lowell's observation was confirmed with each year that Masters lived as an alien exile in the obscure Hotel Chelsea, in New York City. There was nothing in the present to make him rejoice. New York City was one of "noise," "dust," "rattle," and "polyglot confusion." Third Avenue, with "its hot doorways in the summer," "(its) poor hanging out of windows in stifling midnights," "(its) wandering witless men and women wandering the streets,"[9] was a far cry from the prairie America of "days magically lived."

Masters often fled New York for his beloved Middle West, to visit his relatives and to renew himself by breathing prairie air. On one such occasion, on September 3, 1936, his "heart's home" Petersburg honored him by allowing him to read a paper on the courthouse square, at its Centennial Celebration. In this speech Masters, now sixty-seven years old, distilled the essence of his Populism, which heretofore had been spread out in millions of words over a series of decades:

> But if anything can save America it will be the Petersburg idea and conception of life. Here is seed corn saved over from the good days, which if planted and prospered will restore the land. What we need is the old Americanism, never fully tried, and which therefore never failed. The American idea, by which I mean self-reliance, courage, integrity, health of mind and body, industry, thrift, happiness is what we need. Let other lands have what they will, Fascism, Sovietism, Communism. I don't believe in interfering with the business of other lands. But let us stick to the American idea.

Masters was ever an enthusiastic proselytizer, even of fellow Chicagoans who agreed heartily with him. One summer he invited Theodore Dreiser to see and know a remnant of the real America. Masters thought he had succeeded, for he wrote: "John Armstrong obliged the writin' man with stories of Lincoln's day and fiddlin' Turkey in the Straw." With the advent

64

of Masters' seventies, his pessimism softened, yielding to a growing nostalgia until his mind disengaged itself from the present completely in favor of America's golden past. In 1941, he published *Illinois Poems*, which revealed that his convictions remained as strong as ever:

> These hills will tell
> For centuries to come about the land
> About that good America, before the Land
> Of hate, corruption turned life into hell.
>
> "Illinois Ozarks"

Once more the old pioneers are sung:

> Remembering patient women and sturdy men,
> And woodland children, who in laughing health
> Knew neither want nor wealth
> Nor how the city is a stifling den.
>
> "Flowers of Illinois"

Masters closed the volume with a poem expressing the hope that America, diverted from its true path by greed and wrath, would be commanded by the voice to a vision of the Sandridge land.

Along the Illinois followed in 1942, and the publication of this final volume of poetry "only a few miles from Spoon River," gave Masters much satisfaction. Again, the poems are saturated with nostalgia. There was old Jeminie Miles, whose soul has never fled the land he worked though his wagon shed is gone, his barn is ready to topple, and rumors of war (World War II) vex the town ("Old Jeminie Miles"). Expressing excessive nostalgia are such poems as "Going to Atterbury," "Migratory Birds," "Recurring Visions of the Moon," "River Towns," "Orchards in Summer," and "Oak Trees." In "The Prairie: Sandridge," Masters echoed what Bryan had said almost half a century before in his apostrophe to the farm lands of America:

No lesson can be learned: The ancient wars
Corruptions, thefts, degenerating the mind
Have no instructions now, none saving this:
Man cannot ruin the good earth.

Masters simultaneously published *The Sangamon* for the
Rivers of America Series. Here he recapitulated his family history and the oft told story of his own life. All the village
worthies have due note in this volume: Squire Davis Masters,
Hardin Masters, Jack Kelso, and Mentor Graham, a memor-
able school teacher, of whom it is recorded that "one of Lindsay's last poems was about him." Others who appear are
"Doggie Dawson," the farmer, and John Armstrong, the wrest-
ler and fiddler, who had met Theodore Dreiser. A tribute is
paid to Lindsay, and John P. Altgeld is defended once more.
The Sangamon River is made the symbol of the best in
American rivers:

> The Sangamon River! Not navigable, not noted for
> its commercial activity, nor distinguished for majestic
> scenery, nor for a battle, nor for a single historical event,
> distinguished for nothing but for good and useful lives
> lived along its shores, and for the beauty of its prairies
> that sleep and bloom and wave their grasses to the pass-
> ing winds.

Finally Bill McNamar is called,

> the genius of life itself. . . . I believe that Bill never
> learned to read and write, so it was that he didn't have
> to keep up with the flow of books, which do flow and
> pass for good and accomplish nothing.

The final six years of Masters' life were consumed by senil-
ity and ill-health. Some of his correspondence shows him keeping in touch with his contemporaries who, like himself, were
also old and declining. These included Rex Beach, Walter
Trumbull, Gertrude Atherton, and Percy Mackaye.

Stories circulated to the effect that Masters was poverty-stricken and ill in a charity hospital. It would have been a fitting close to Masters' life to claim that America, which he loved and for which he desired the best, had given him the hemlock as it had Vachel Lindsay and William Marion Reedy. But, a curmudgeon to the end, Masters vehemently denied the poverty.[10] Neverthless, when Masters died six years later, *Time Magazine* in its obituary circulated the story of poverty and hunger:

> Accusing the United States of ingratitude to poets Masters was found broke, ill and half-starved in Manhattan in 1944, two years later (he) was given a $5,000 fellowship by the Academy of American Poets.

Bernard De Voto has called Masters a "Delphic Apollo in an Illinois river bottom" characterized by "frequent McGuffey rant" and "frequent McGuffey idealism." Fred B. Millet has rated *Spoon River Anthology* as "a landmark in the history of contemporary poetry." Professor Percy H. Boynton has decided that Masters

> lost his way in total irresolution. He was neither classicist nor modernist, lawyer nor poet, poet nor prose writer, novelist nor biographer, Chicagoan nor New Yorker.

The consensus of criticism is that Edgar Lee Masters will be remembered for his *Spoon River Anthology*. Nevertheless, a new critical estimate of Masters, based on his voluminous writings rather than on one or two works, is called for at this time.

The forty years of Edgar Lee Masters' literary production show little change in his original principles, prejudices, attitudes, and nostalgias. Wisely or unwisely, he remained constant to his primary themes, and any changes that occurred did not affect his fundamental beliefs. Certain convictions deepened, particularly his assurance that America was decadent and corrupt, and that its glories lay in the past: a past whose return he alternately despaired of and hoped for.

Significant in the changes that did occur in his thought were his increasing skepticism concerning political idealism and his enfeebled belief in "the people." His poems, in fact, betrayed the weakness of the Populist position generally. Like the Populists, he was against many things, and he was strong, even acid, in his denunciations. But the positive content of his poetry, save when he was celebrating the past, was negligible.

Masters' "nay-saying" was in conformity with the protesting spirit of Populism. He was well aware of the criticism and ridicule leveled at the ineffective politics of the Populists. His rebuttal was:

> The old days there was enormous chatter about historic Democracy and about Populist confusion and enervation. But if Populism so-called was a disaster, has Wall Street been a success? It never has been and never can be while the Democratic party remains an agrarian party—that is, while it stands opposed to laws which build up commerce and manufacturing at the expense of agriculture and divert the natural cause of wealth and its production.

From this viewpoint he never wavered, and though he recognized that the Republican Party and the Democratic Party were too often identical in their support of a strong federal government and the moneyed powers, he chose to support the Democratic Party since that was the agrarian party, the party of the South.

H. L. Mencken, Masters' friend, clearly saw Masters' chief weakness when he said, "most of the Spoon River poems are tracts, and many of them are very bad tracts." But even more damaging was Masters' lack of the poetic gift, which we have noted elsewhere. After decades of versification and hundreds of thousands of lines of verse, Masters failed to grow as a poet—remaining as much an imitator and novice at the end of his career as he had been when he published his *Book of Verses* in 1898.

The Spoon River Anthology was an accident. This writer has no doubt that Masters intended his original *Spoon River* poems as a crude satire upon the uncouth productions of the *vers-librists*. This was the opinion of people on the Chicago literary scene, and Masters himself hinted at the truth when he confessed to Hamlin Garland that *Spoon River* was foreign to him and rationalized "which only shows with many of us, if not with all, we do not what we dream, but what something beyond or over us dictates."[11] Masters' success with the *Anthology*, his acceptance by Harriet Monroe into her *Poetry Magazine* circle, the friendship and encouragement of Sandburg and other *vers-librists* confounded him. He longed to be a poet of the old vintage, using poetic diction, invoking the Muses and the Gods, writing apostrophes to animate Nature, and striving for the sublime. Consequently, rather than choosing *vers-libre* which might have been more suitable to his talents, Masters emphasized "the classical." The result was a dichotomy in language and subject matter which made Masters appear to be two different writers. On the one hand he wrote Americana; on the other hand he composed poor imitations of formal verse, from Homer to his own day.

Masters was basically a prose man, but his craving to achieve recognition as a poet, along with his political propaganda and prejudices, and his slavery to imitation, vitiated his prose. In the novel, he desired to write another *Huckleberry Finn* and *Tom Sawyer*. He merely succeeded in being a *petit Twain*, while professional mediocrities wrote of Main Street America and reaped the recognition and the sales. In biography, Masters' prepossessions precluded work of any value, with the exception of his biography of Vachel Lindsay, whom he knew and to whose papers he had access. Better biographies of Lindsay will undoubtedly appear, but, while Masters' biography has already drawn the criticism from many quarters that it is inaccurate and that it reveals Masters rather than Lindsay, it will always remain a valuable source book.

Finally, while American literature is still young and its writers of stature remain limited in numbers, some of Masters' *Spoon River Poems* will appear in literary histories and in anthologies of American poetry. But because Masters 'poems *per se* are not striking, it is more than likely that they will not be read. Anthologies of American poetry have already appeared in which Masters is not represented. Apart from his literary significance, Masters will be of value to the social historian, for he claimed to have "written nothing that was not true to life as he has seen and lived it."

In his fifty odd volumes a panorama of American history appears as seen by a frustrated agrarian sympathizer, who, though he personally could brook neither the village nor the city, fervently wished that America had remained a country of small Jeffersonian villages inhabited by a life-loving, homogeneous, farmer population.

CHAPTER V

VACHEL LINDSAY

Springfield Beginnings

In a letter to Louis Untermeyer, Lindsay, having stated that he had spent half a day with Masters, continued:

> I find Masters very congenial and expect to find him more so. We have a heap in common with our forebears and themes—and I think we can see a parallelism between the Village Magazine and the Anthology though he leans towards the wets and I lean towards the drys.[12]

This seeing a parallelism was perceptive criticism by Lindsay, who, though ten years younger than Masters, had been old enough in his formative years to be influenced by the Populism of the day, and who was to become "one of its great voices."

Lindsay was proud of his grandfather, E. S. Frazee, of Rush County, Indiana, from whom he acquired his agrarian and Jeffersonian Protestantism. "Grandpa Frazee" was a pioneer, with the proportions of an epic hero:

Into the acres of the newborn state
He poured his strength, and plowed his ancient name,
And, when traders followed him, he stood
Towering above their furtive souls and tame.

71

That brow without a stain, that fearless eye
Oft left the passing stranger wondering
To find such knighthood in the sprawling land,
To see a democrat well-nigh a king.

He lived with liberal hand, with guests from far,
With talk and joke and fellowship to spare—
Watching the wide world's life from sun to sun,
Lining his walls with books from everywhere.

He read at night, he built his world by day.
The farm and house of God to him were one.
For forty years he preached and plowed and wrought—
A statesman in the fields, who bent to none.

His plowmen—neighbours were as lords to him.
His was an ironside democratic pride.
He served a rigid Christ, but served him well—
And, for a lifetime, saved the countryside . . .

"The Proud Farmer"

All the tenets of the Populist cult of the pioneer are here:
the pioneer is noble, hard-working, a lover of clean, simple fun,
impeccably democratic. Jack Kelso apart, Lindsay's pioneer
differs from Masters' pioneer in that he is a "reading" and a
religious man. His farmland is a temple, and the Republic, "the
countryside," is safe as long as the pioneer exists. But the suc-
cessors to the pioneer are the corrupting traders whose souls
are "furtive and tame."

Lindsay's pride in the past by no means excluded his grandmother:

And I back my one drop of blood
From this Indian girl
Against all the blood of the Normans,
Where the British flags unfurl.

"The Indian Girl—My Grandmother"

Every summer Lindsay visited these grandparents at their Indiana farm, where he heard tales of pioneers and listened to the talk of farmers. Adding to this agrarian background were Lindsay's parents, both Kentuckians steeped in the tradition of the agrarian South. Lindsay's father was a country doctor, a thoroughly good man, devoted to his profession; a prohibitionist, unalterably opposed to liquor, tobacco, dancing, and card playing. His mother was

> an ardent temperance worker, a Sunday-school teacher, and the founder and first president of the Union of Women's Missionary Societies of all the churches of Springfield.

Both parents were members of the Campbellite Church, the "Disciples Church." And Campbell, the founder of this church, was Populistic in his preachments:

> He preached with faultless logic
> An American Millennium:
> The social order
> Of a realist and farmer
> With every neighbor
> Within stone wall and border.
> "A Rhymed Address to All Renegade Campbellites"

Lindsay's acceptance of the religious tradition passed on to him by his parents, despite its narrowness and its anachronism in the widening horizon of the twentieth century, reveals that Lindsay was a traditionalist at heart, ready to adhere to the values he had learned as a boy. His father was said never to have forgiven Lincoln for the Civil War; and while Lindsay did not sympathize with Dr. Lindsay as regards that hatred, he did venerate the South, and he did consider himself a Southerner.

> Why do I faint with love
> Till the prairies dip and reel?
> My heart is a kicking horse
> Shod with Kentucky steel.

No drop of my blood from north
Of Mason and Dixon's Line.

"My Father Came From Kentucky"

Lindsay also regarded himself as a Virginian. "You may rage
and roar; but you cannot destroy the gauntlet, the bonnet and
the plume. These are part of Thomas Jefferson's thousand
years."

The Civil War had severely injured the Lindsay family:

> Slaves had been taken away; fertile farm lands had been
> lost in the Carpet-Bag era; and members of the family
> accustomed to the riches and culture of the old leisurely
> South were reduced to a life of poverty.

The agrarian Lindsays migrated to the farmlands of Illinois, as
had other Southerners like Squire Davis Masters, giving the
Middle West a Southern cast.

Lindsay regarded the place of his birth, Springfield, as a
Southern town, claiming emphatically: "For better or for worse
it *is* a Southern town." The house in which Lindsay was born
had been owned by Abraham Lincoln's sister-in-law; adjacent
to it was the Illinois Executive Mansion, of considerable importance in Lindsay's development.

Lindsay was fully aware of the decisive influence of those
early years: "I was born in Springfield, Illinois, in the house
where I now live. Everything begins and ends there for me."
Springfield became for Lindsay an ideal, representative of
America at her best, and a way of life:

> I believe profoundly in our agricultural and middle
> west civilization and think it is the natural America, and
> the America with oldest and most normal history. I greatly
> mistrust Industrial America, radical or conservative . . . I
> am keenly aware of how I differ from everything east of
> the Mississippi River.[13]

74

Just as Hardin Masters served as a delegate to the Democratic presidential convention, so, too, did Dr. Lindsay. And though only a boy at the time, Lindsay was one of the crowd who thronged round the State House at Springfield to hear Bryan.

William Jennings Bryan became one of Lindsay's heroes. For him Bryan was not only a statesman but a poet, a super-poet, capable of reaching American audiences of one million or one hundred million by a mere "tent" speech. It was from Bryan that Lindsay acquired his "crusading-spirit," his favorite war cry remaining "Rah for Bryan!" Bryan's manner of speaking also impressed Lindsay, who imitated it, and, most important, Byran inspired one of Lindsay's best poems, which Edward Davison has ranked as his best single poem.

The poem, "Bryan, Bryan, Bryan, Bryan," plus its lengthy sub-title, "The Campaign of Eighteen-Ninety-Six, as viewed at the time by a Sixteen-Year-old, etc.," speaks for itself:

I

. . . .

I brag and chant of Bryan, Bryan, Bryan
 Candidate for president who sketched a
silver Zion . . .

It was eighteen ninety-six, and I was just sixteen
And Altgeld ruled in Springfield, Illinois,
When there came from the sunset Nebraska's
shout of joy;
In a coat like a deacon, in a black Stetson hat
He scourged the elephant plutocrats
With barbed wire from the Platte . . .

II

And all these in their helpless days
. . . .
By the dour East oppressed,

Mean paternalism
Making their mistakes for them
Crucifying half the West
Till the whole Atlantic coast
Seemed a giant spiders' nest.

III

. . . .

And Bryan took the platform
And he was introduced.
And he lifted his hand
And cast a new spell.
Progressive silence fell
In Springfield,
In Illinois,
Around the world.
Then we heard these boulders across
the prairie rolled:
*"The People have a right to make their
own mistakes . . .
You shall not crucify mankind
Upon a cross of gold.*

IV

. . . .

Then Hanna came to the rescue,
Hanna of Ohio,
Rallying the roller-tops
Rallying the bucket-shops.
Threatening drouth and death,
Promising manna,
Rallying the trusts against the bawling
flannel mouth;
Invading misers' cellars,
Tin-cans, socks,
Melting down the rocks,

Pouring out the long green to a million
workers,
Spondulix by the mountain-load, to stop
each new tornado,
And beat the cheapskate, blatherskite,
Populistic, anarchistic,
Deacon-desperado.

V

Election night by midnight:
Boy Bryan's defeat.
Defeat of western silver.
Defeat of the wheat . . . .

The fact that Lindsay still idolized Bryan long after the latter's stature had shrunk to pitiful proportions reveals the impact Bryan had had on Lindsay. In 1915, nearly twenty years after Bryan's defeat, when so many had found cause to revise their earlier estimates of Bryan, Lindsay wrote a poem eulogizing him

When Bryan speaks, the sky is ours
The wheat, the forests, and the flowers
And who is here to say us nay
Fled are the ancient tyrant powers.

When Bryan speaks, then I rejoice
His is the strange composite voice
Of many million singing souls
Who make world-brotherhood their choice.

Nothing that Bryan himself did, nor any criticism, succeeded in causing Lindsay to change his mind. When Edgar Lee Masters attacked Byran in "The Cocked Hat," Lindsay, acknowledging in the margin that "The Cocked Hat" had made the "most marked impression" on him, expressed the view that Bryan had shown courage on the peace issue of World War I.

Lindsay admitted that he had a "weakness" for Bryan, the "democratic pipe organ"; and in *The Litany of Washington Street*, Lindsay went so far as to call the Middle West "the Bryan farms."

John P. Altgeld did not exercise the same profound and decisive influence, but he was another of the great heroes of the Middle West from whom Lindsay acquired the beliefs and prejudices that shaped him. Lindsay included Altgeld in his "secular hagiography of America," without following Masters' example of exalting Altgeld by deprecating Bryan. It was to Altgeld's inspiration that he owed "The Eagle That Is Forgotten." Lindsay wrote exultantly to Jessie B. Rittenhouse:

> Do you know the story of the Altgeld poem and all that went into it, and the long history before it, almost amounts to a romance now? One spectacle after another in his big life and my small one—I will tell you of it when we meet. I could write a book upon that man. The triumph of the poem, such as it is, is a kind of triumph few enthusiasts get so soon for their hobbies or lost causes.

Miss Rittenhouse's assertion that it was Altgeld who turned Lindsay's "thoughts into national channels and socialized his point of view" is strongly supported by Lindsay's letter and by the reverence for Altgeld revealed in the poem's closing stanza, the most reverent lines Lindsay ever wrote:

> Sleep softly . . . eagle forgotten . . . under
> the stone,
> Time has its way with you there and the
> day its own.
> Sleep on, O brave-hearted, O wise man,
> that kindled the flame—
> To live in mankind is far more than to
> live in a name,
> To live in mankind, far, far more . . . than
> to live in a name.
> "The Eagle That Is Forgotten"

Lindsay emulated Edgar Lee Masters' example of inserting Altgeld's name in various poems, an expedient adopted to do it honor and to keep it alive. In "In Memory of a Good Printer," one of the points Lindsay makes in favor of his subject is that he had printed "proud Altgeld's word without disgrace." Altgeld's name appears several times in "Bryan, Bryan, Bryan, Bryan," where Lindsay asks passionately:

> Where is Altgeld, brave as truth
> Whose name the few still say with tears?

Lindsay answers that Altgeld the Eagle now rests in the shadows with "Heaven-born Bryan," "Homer Bryan, who sang from the West."

The Development of Lindsay's Mind

The actual development of Lindsay's political thought is not easy to trace, a fact which might explain why so many students of Lindsay have reached such different conclusions regarding his beliefs and ideas. Lindsay, alive to this, insisted on chronology, evidently believing that the guidance thus provided would serve as a guard against error. He wrote:

> But bear in mind that my tramp days were mixed with the rest. I walked in the South in the spring of 1906, in the East in the spring of 1908, and in the West in the spring of 1912. There is a very definite progress of ideas in the accounts of these regions. Please remember "The Handy Guide for Beggars" begins the story. People get so very wide of the mark I am perhaps getting finicky on this matter of chronology.

In the decade bridged by the years 1896 to the spring of 1906 Lindsay lived from his sixteenth to his twenty-sixth year. The decade opened with the momentous Populist election, which marked the defeat of Bryan, "defeat of my boyhood, defeat of my dreams." Poetically, the decade was not fruitful as far as Lindsay was concerned, and the period can only be described as one of rather uneventful growth. He graduated from Springfield High School in 1897, and then he attended Hiram College, a Campellite college.

Lindsay was not a success in formal education, failing so many courses that after three years he was still not beyond sophomore standing. In 1900 Lindsay left Hiram, without taking a degree, and without any desire to renew his assault on "higher" education. He willingly confessed that "he could not get a diploma in twenty years."[14]

This failure in formal education could not have disturbed him as much as a success would have, for the egalitarianism of Populism brooked no pretensions to intellectual superiority— all men were equal. Nevertheless, Lindsay, in a moment of self-satisfaction with his occupation of itinerant lecturer, considered the co-educational, denominational colleges like Hiram and Baylor University "the highest point in American civilization." However, Populist influence led Lindsay to feel that there was something European about America's best universities, those of the East.

> They are not as completely the flower of America as are the co-educational religious schools, which grow up out of the ground as naturally as the blue grass and the Indian corn and the violets.

Consistently Lindsay's opinion of finishing schools was unfavorable:

> They are from first to last for one purpose, to teach young girls to be outrageous, subtle, and effective snobs, and they have little excuses for being.

Finally he regarded "scholarship" with scorn: "When men work for high degrees in the universities, they labor on a piece of literary conspiracy called a thesis which no one outside the university hears of again."

80

Lindsay could substantiate his prejudice; for years, he earned his livelihood by lecturing in colleges and women's clubs across the country, and his reception reinforced his contempt for his "educated" audiences. Again and again, with mass vulgarity and without having taken the pains to read some of his work, they insisted that he should recite one of his popular poems such as "The Congo," "General Booth Enters Heaven," or "The Santa Fe Trail." Growing to hate this, Lindsay wrote to Louis Untermeyer:

> (It) will drive me mad if I do them once more. The public positively clamors for them and absolutely refuses to listen to my new pieces. Yet they stand me up to recite till I am sick of my life.[15]

Finally, in a moment of ruthless self-examination, he saw his lecturing to the "educated" as so much wasted time:

> I am through with the educational world as such. I want to get right down now to the man in the street, and pepper him till he is as crazy to go to the book store as to the Ford Emporium.

Lindsay's further contempt for universities and university people was revealed in an article in *The Saturday Evening Post*, where he questioned

> the frame of mind of the university which would send for a poet three times in three different years to cross a thousand miles of desert merely to gaze on him without once buying one of his books.

In January, 1901, Lindsay went to Chicago where he began to study art at the Art Institute, leaving there for New York, where he continued his studies at The Art Students' League. These were years of poverty and odd jobs, and they were also years in which Lindsay first announced parts of his "message," lecturing at a Y.M.C.A. in New York and for the Anti-Saloon League in Illinois.

The year 1906 was one of decisive importance in Lindsay's life; he set out as a tramp poet, his poetry as slender as his immediate means of subsistence. Having taken a steamer passage to Florida, he found himself stranded in Jacksonville with only five cents in his pocket. He recalled his experiences with an evident relish:

> It was not till March 1906 that I made the plunge being stranded in Florida with malice aforethought. I tramped. I rode freight. I rode freight cabooses two hundred miles, then tramped again eight hundred miles through Macon and Atlanta, Georgia; Ashville, North Carolina; Greenville, Tennessee; and Cumberland Gap to Frankfort, Kentucky. My baggage was a razor, toothbrush, comb, soap, bandana, and my poem "The Tree of Laughing Bells." I found an extraordinary responsiveness in cultured and uncultured. It seemed the only time I had ever lived. I will never forget those log houses of the Blue Ridge, those rings of faces lit only by the fire in the hearth.

This first wandering set the mold for Lindsay's later life and thought, for it served to reaffirm hs Bryanism and his belief in the common people. "The Man under the Yoke," who gave Lindsay shelter, "had nothing, and gave me half of it and we both had an abundance." This samaritan, who provided Lindsay with such a happy encounter, was "what I came out into the wilderness to see." Significantly, Lindsay does not omit to mention that his samaritan was a victim of "big money":

> His bosses in the lumber camp kept his wages down to the point where the grocery bills took all his pay, thus forcing him to trade at the 'company' store, there in the heart of the pine woods.

In Atlanta, Georgia, Lindsay found himself without money and he was accorded the shelter of the Salvation Army for three nights. There a "religious leader" evinced a desire to argue with Lindsay:

> He denounced labor agitators in plain words. I agreed. I belong to the brotherhood of those who loaf and invite their souls.
> He spoke of anarchy. I maintained that I loved the law. He very clearly, and at length, assaulted *Single Tax*. I knew nothing then of Single Tax, and thanked him for light. He denounced Socialism. Knowing little about Socialism at that time, I denounced it also, having just been converted to individualism by a man in the Highlands.

Though at that time Lindsay was on much safer ground when speaking of farming and hogs, he became both a single taxer and, despite the wayfarer's denunciations, a Socialist also. Later he moved away from the isolationist aspects of Byranism to become an internationalist. These changes in Lindsay's attitudes and beliefs explain why he insisted on "chronology."

"The Tree of Laughing Bells," or "The Wings of the Morning" referred to above, was a long nature poem dedicated to "aviators," with echoes of Edgar Allan Poe, Byron, Keats, Shelley, and Swinburne. Lindsay had published it as a broadside at his own expense in 1905, and the following year, he traded it with whoever would accept it for food and shelter. The poem dealt with an Indian Maid, but not an Indian Maid of the "wild" West. This is ethereal Indian maid such as is found in Shelley and Keats, but despite her celestial nature, Lindsay's localism appears in this early poem.

> These, the Wings of Morning
> An Indian Maiden wove
> Intertwining subtlely
> Wands from a willow grove
> Beside the Sangamon—
> Rude stream of Dreamland Town.

Lindsay had begun making a mythic stream of the Sangamon before he met Masters. Frequently he introduced into his poems and prose the name of the sluggish river that ran through Sangamon County, Illinois. "Three fairies by the Sangamon were dancing for a prize," he wrote in one poem, and in another poem he had a Dryad-inhabited tree grow from Sangamon earth. Thus Clara Stocker was right when she described the Sangamon as "Vachel's favorite stream."

Lindsay's tramp also reinforced his Populist belief that cities and technology did not represent America or Art. When the man "in the city of collars" asked Lindsay, who was trying to exchange a poem for a new collar, why he tramped about, Lindsay answered sternly, "Art, my friend, does not travel in a Pullman." Industrial America aroused his indignation: "Oil City is an ugly, confused kind of place. There are thousands like it in the United States." Henceforth Lindsay never wearied of calling attention to his belief that cities were ugly and that progress was meaningless.

Lindsay's Populism found expression in the first three of the eight rules he formulated for himself when out tramping:

1. Keep away from the cities.
2. Keep away from the railroads.
3. Have nothing to do with money.
   Carry no baggage.

Lindsay was intelligent enough to realize that his economic position as a tramp was not generally acceptable, but he was determined to belong to "the leisure classes, which rhymers belong to." He rationalized his position in a far from novel manner: "In order to belong to any leisure class, one must be a thief or a beggar. On the whole I prefer to be a beggar." This rejection of material accumulation was a far cry from the success myth of America.

Inevitably Lindsay advocated the artist's abandoning of civilization, a pronunciamento in accord with the Populist belief that the frontier farms and open roads were the avenues of the real America:

The spiritual necessity for leaving behind railroads and cities cannot be overstated. They blight those fine things in the soul which this discipline of ours is presumed to upbuild. . . . He who would bring the new moods to our time, and a new civilization, must not place himself where he will be overwhelmed by the contraptions of the old.

This hatred of cities and industrialism received its ultimate expression in Lindsay. In 1909, in one of his "War Bulletins," which he published at his own expense, Lindsay exhorted:

Let us enter the great offices and shut the desk lids and cut telephone wires. Let us see that the skyscrapers are empty and locked and the keys thrown into the river. Let us break up the cities. Let us send men on a great immigration: set free, purged of the commerce-made manners and fat prosperity of America; ragged with the beggars' pride, starving with the crusader's fervor. Better to die of the plague on the highroad, seeing angels, than live on iron streets playing checkers with dollars forever and ever.

This desire for the destruction of "metropolized" America was not capricious iconoclasm on Lindsay's part; he reiterated it three years later as "a speech he didn't make" in a magazine article for national consumption:

Let us preach the divine freedom of poverty till the skyscrapers are empty and locked and keys thrown in the ocean. Let us preach the gospel of going afoot till there shall be neither tramps in boxcars nor aristocrats in Pullman cars. Let us persuade men to turn their backs on the railroads till it becomes a thread of rust. Let us lead forth a great pedestrian immigration, set free, purged of the commerce-made manners and fat prosperity of America. . . .

Since the pulverization of the cities was not likely to occur Lindsay tried to "save" them with religious ritual, and one of his tracts was significantly entitled: "The Soul of the City Receives the Gift of the Holy Spirit." This tract which he called "programme one" and "the index to all my writing," he issued in 1912, after a trip across Kansas, distributing several thousand copies in his beloved Springfield. It was illustrated with drawings, ten of them symbolic. One drawing called "The Village Improvement Parade," has in it banners with such legends as: "Fair Streets are Better than Silver; Green Parks are Better than Gold." "Bad taste is Mob-Law; Good Public Taste is Democracy." "Ugliness is a kind of Misgovernment." "A Bad Designer is to That Extent, A Bad Citizen."

Several cities came under Lindsay's censure. San Francisco, "The City That Will Not Repent," is, in Lindsay's poem, loved by God though it "Scorns and blasphemes him strong." Evidently torn between his hatred of cities and his religious sense of salvation, Lindsay warns that God may have to send down flame upon San Francisco to please his angels. In a long poem, "So Much the Worse for Boston," Lindsay has nothing good to say for that city. Similarly, he told an interviewer: "New York is the vest pocket of America. But though it may set the time for the country, it isn't the country." In his poetry Lindsay warned that people should not be misled by skyscrapers, and he encouraged those without hope to "turn to the little prairie towns." Nevertheless he was fearful lest Springfield become "metropolized" as had Spoon River.

> Let not our town be large, remembering
> That little Athens was the Muses' home
> That Oxford rules the heart of London still
> That Florence gave the Renaissance to Rome.

"A Gospel of Beauty: III On the Building of Springfield"

Lindsay found it easy to denounce cities, not only because of his natural provincial's dislike of the city and Bryan's fiery "Cross-of-Gold" speech, but also because of his religious nature. Lindsay confessed that he had "tried many Gods," and in Lindsay's religions there was much that was consonant with

Populism, and rather than one obscuring the other, they were complementary. The brotherhood of man, the pacifist injunction, "thou shalt not kill," money and cities as instruments of evil, the wholesomeness of the hard, frugal life—all these ideas appeared in Lindsay's religious beliefs, variable and eclectic though they might have been.

Lindsay's Tolerance and Intolerance

Lindsay had much more reason than Masters to hate the East, particularly New York, for he had been accorded a chill reception in the city:

> All the doors were closed to me in New York . . . I was buffeted and beaten. . . . I could not even secure an opening on a newspaper. But I found there were people who would not let me go hungry—that was out on the open road.

Lindsay was, indeed, buffeted and beaten:

> He besieged publishers with his just completed book, *Aladdin's Lamp*, hand-printed and beautifully illustrated, containing the germs of most of his later poems, but the publishers would have none of it.

He destroyed the book when his mother grieved that art was leading the entire family astray. Even after Lindsay had achieved fame he suffered not only the humiliation of rejection, but, according to William Cabell Greet, one commercial concern, which Lindsay had approached concerning the making of some records, rebuffed him "in a very cruel manner."

Churlish treatment and indifference did not inspire any racial or nationalist hostility in Lindsay, who, during his tramping days, had often encountered rabid racists and had listened intently to their theories. He had set down the peculiar racist ideas one man had offered to him:

A Japanese is a nigger. . . . The white people ought to keep their blood pure. Russians are white people. Germans, English, and Americans are white people. French people are niggers. Dagoes are niggers. Jews are niggers. All people are niggers but just those four.

Curiously for one who was so clearly a humanitarian, Lindsay never condemned the racists. Perhaps he thought that their opinions were so ludicrous that they would reveal themselves for what they were if he simply set them down. He did, however, write in clear terms what he thought of foreigners for the benefit of his "fellow-Babbits":

In the railroad cutting down near the bridge the Italians are blasting the rock. Some day you will use the railroad. . . .
The Lithuanians are digging in a mine just two miles away. They are blowing themselves to pieces all that you may have coal in the cellar and a warm Reception Room.

Edgar Lee Masters, as we have noted, accused the Jews of the publishing trade of discriminating against Lindsay, but if the charge had substance, it did not provoke Lindsay into denouncing such treatment, and it did not inspire in him the least taint of anti-Semitism. On the contrary, in his search for a God who would satisfy his intellectual and emotional needs, he did not hesitate to adopt for a time Yahweh, the God of the Jews. He corresponded with Rabbi Stephen S. Wise, who had, Lindsay recorded, "several times made friendly motions in my direction," [16] and he recited some of his poetry for Rabbi Wise's synagogue. Lindsay wrote of "the brilliant Jew from the bleeding Ghettos of Russia" who came to the United States to give it the beauty of his violin, and he regarded the publication of his *The Chinese Nightingale and Other Poems* by the Macmillan Company of New York as "a tribute to the Jewish race." [17]

If he noticed anything unworthy in the Jews, the Irish, Poles or Italians, he regarded it as due to their city and industrial environment, rather than to any peculiarity in their make-up as a race or people. This is evident in a lecture which he delivered in the fall of 1908, under the auspices of the Young Men's Christian Association. In this he pleaded that, instead of making policemen of the Irish, fruit vendors of the Italians, and coal-miners of the Poles, each group should be allowed to develop its particular genius. "If they have contributed to European civilization, why not let them contribute to ours instead of enslaving them to our industrialism?"

Lindsay's egalitarianism also included the American Negro, for though he insisted he was a Southerner and though Springfield was a Southern town in that it had a Negro population and the usual prejudices against the Negro, Lindsay achieved his own democratic attitude. He regarded the Negro with an unfailing sympathy and felt ashamed of Negro persecution. In this tolerance he was in accord with the Southern Populists, who had demanded equal rights for Negroes. As "The Booker T. Washington Trilogy" reveals, Lindsay did not hesitate to honor the Negro in his poetry, and if the whites regarded his Negro sermon poems as funny, Lindsay was deadly serious about them. Finally the degree of Lindsay's seriousness concerning the Negro was expressed in the view that, if he had to fight in a war he "would rather die for the 'poor nigger' than any other breed of man."

Just as Lindsay was unable to share Edgar Lee Masters' anti-racial prejudices, neither could he share Masters' Anglophobia. He did not regard England as the sinister imperialist nation from whom America learned her imperialism. In 1920, Chatto and Windus, the London publishers, brought out his *General Booth* volume "with a generous introduction by Robert Nichols," and in the same year he took his mother along for a "triumphant visit to England." When J. C. Squire, the Englishman, was about to visit New York, Lindsay wrote to Untermeyer: "I am very eager for you and your group to have no prejudices when he lands in New York in January. Squire is the most ultra-English person I have ever met. [18]

Lindsay's admirable tolerance of all races and creeds and his religious charity excluded two classes found in America, two classes associated with a preoccupation with money—millionaires and "Babbitts." The former he referred to as "mutt millionaires,"[19] and he thought that their money should be used for worthy causes. In one instance he wondered whether some dying mogul "gorged with ill-earned M(otion) P(icture) money" might not like Carnegie with his "penitential libraries" and Rockefeller with his "penitential University," endow a museum for the then infant movie industry. His use of the word "gorged," with its connotation of swinishness and, of the word "penitential," with its connotation of sin requiring penance reveals his attitude toward wealth.

The Babbitt, the businessman of twentieth century America, who had become the vulgar arbiter of American social, political and artistic life, drew Lindsay's special fire. Lindsay had a very clear conception of what he meant by Babbitt and Babbittry:

> Babbittry is simply the state of mind of the small American businessman of Main Street. The men who are his bosses are not Babbitts. And neither are the laboring men and the farmers.

Lindsay felt immune to the contagion of Babbittry, for he could not even imagine himself as a businessman. But, when he saw Indians "dressed for war, yet dancing for a Babbitt jamboree," anger rose in him. Nor did he choose to conceal his anger and contempt; he preferred to ridicule the Babbitts of Springfield in the person of "John Fletcher, A Doubter":

> He is a high authority in the financial circles of Springfield. He is religious on Sundays only, from eleven till twelve-thirty, when he sits in his pew. . . . He is quite sure the Emancipation Proclamation meant that millionaires are exempt from criticism. . . . He is quite sure that anyone who protests against his views is a "red." And "red," "radical," "anarchist" and "liberal" are absolutely synonymous, according to his thinking. He is sure that anyone who does not want to be a millionaire is contemplating

arson. He is quite sure that every large bank account is automatically moral, and that every small one is almost moral, and that the one crime is to be without money.

Lindsay's indignation evaporated only under the satisfying thought that Babbitt's day was "surely past" and under the enigmatic conviction that "the Virginians are coming again."

Lindsay's Political Heroes and Politics

In his approach to history Lindsay differed markedly from Masters; Lindsay believed not in a "money" theory but in a "romantic theory." According to this theory poets and artists were to be elected to power, an accomplishment which called for Machiavellian subtlety:

> In economics we can put them all to sleep and off their guard by being as conservative as the Pope of Rome. But once the Poets and Artists are in power, goodbye to the businessmen and tariff senators and such forever more.

And in view of this romantic theory it is pertinent to examine Lindsay's attitudes toward historical and contemporary personages, as we did with Masters.

Lindsay's attitude toward George Washington was mixed; on the one hand he could see the three superb horsemen, Washington, Jefferson, and Hamilton, riding abreast, the "Virginians" of "the gauntlet, the bonnet and the plume"; on the other hand Washington's "grand style" offended his Populist sensibilities—Washington was not one of the people, and "Washington Street," Lindsay wrote, "is forever Against Main Street," a statement which is illuminated elsewhere:

> Andrew Jackson showed that sound instinct in fighting Washington. There was something in it deeper than politics. Andrew Jackson foresaw the two-cent stamp, and the Gilbert Stuart portraits. The only direct imitation of

George Washington's grand style I know is Robert E. Lee.
I prefer J. E. B. Stuart, as a hero of the Confederacy.

Therefore, when Lindsay wrote that the Constitution was "cut
to fit the pattern of George Washington," it can be inferred
that the Constitution was not as democratic a document as
Lindsay would have wished.

There was nothing ambiguous in Lindsay's attitude toward
Thomas Jefferson, the source of many of Lindsay's beliefs.
For Lindsay, the soul of Jefferson represented the soul of
America. Lindsay was sure that "at the end of a thousand years
Jefferson's ideas will prevail"; and Lindsay could speak readily
in terms of what constituted Jefferson's thousand years. Lindsay was willing to invent myths about his idol. He conjured a
picture of dancers dancing to one tune, played by the only
instrument in the world that had that tune—the violin of
Thomas Jefferson. In a second fantasy Lindsay has a character
called The Ancient Mariner who

> looks into *The Flying Book of Sangamon County* and
> Springfield with *Its Wings and Leaves of Gold*, and plays
> fantastically upon Thomas Jefferson's old Virginia violin
> from its pages. . . .

As Lindsay regarded himself as a "true Jeffersonian," it was
perfectly natural for him to give an oration on Jefferson's birthday at a political banquet of the Democratic Party, where he
experienced great satisfaction in having one of his pieces "accepted definitely as a political oration for a definite party, and
not as a parlor poem." Still Lindsay felt that he had been
inconsistent in his Jeffersonianism. His wanderings particularly
caused him concern in this connection, to such an extent that
he denounced them:

> But it does not behoove the true Jeffersonian American to
> break his home-ties forever and stew away to nothing in
> the far country simply because in his early youth someone
> in authority praised one of his songs. The village poet, the

hometown poet, should rather aspire to an old-age veteranship. . . . If he desires immortality, let it be among the children of his personal friends in his home town. I hope any reader of the *Mirror* who knows a poet that needs this message, will not hesitate to clip it out and send it to him.

Lindsay's reverence for Andrew Jackson was such that he expressed the belief that when the statue of Andrew Jackson was removed from the White House lawn in Washington, America was "doomed." Lindsay wrote:

Andrew Jackson was eight feet tall
His arm was a hickory limb and a maul
His sword was so long he dragged it on
the ground
Every friend was an equal. Every foe
was a hound.

Andrew Jackson was a democrat
Defying Kings in his old cocked hat. . . .
"The Statue of Old Andrew Jackson"

In his worship for Jackson, Lindsay discarded his pacifism, a fact which caused Louis Untermeyer, Lindsay's close friend and confidant, to write that never had patriotism and poetry "so treacherously mixed."

The accusation is just, but this lapse of Lindsay's is explained by the fact that a Lindsay hero can do no wrong. They were immaculate, these Lindsay heroes, and they won his heart and mind so completely that he was quite incapable of detecting in them the slightest flaw. In this connection, Andrew Jackson was without superior in Lindsay's roster of heroes: "I am naturally far more of a Woodrow Wilson and Andrew Jackson Democrat, than a socialist, and more accord with the South than the North in general political ideas." Writing in *The New Republic*, he said: "I prefer Whitman to Longfellow . . . But I prefer Andrew Jackson to either man, as a 'hero.' Here I part with the village." His regard for Jackson found expression in his *Collected Poems*:

> I still thrill to Andrew Jackson's old toast at the famous banquet: "The Federal Union—it must and shall be preserved." But I would alter it to: "The League of Nations, it must and shall be preserved." And in my fancy I see Andrew Jackson rising to propose that toast to the world. Something like this is the implication beneath the prose work, "The Golden Book of Springfield."

In Kerensky's succession to the Czarist despotism he saw "Andrew Jackson liberty, bleeding Kansas liberty." He attributed some of the power in the first and second *Spoon River Anthologies* to the fact that Edgar Lee Masters was "a stern Jacksonian."

In spite of the Lindsay family's losses in the Civil War, Lindsay worshiped Lincoln. This is not to say that Lindsay was a "Northerner," but that he could suspend his Southern agrarianism: "It was the Civil War which hurled Illinois into unity, which centered it around Lincoln. . . ." His attitude toward the Civil War suggests that he accepted it as a necessary evil; his feelings might be summed up in the words he had a Kentucky mountaineer speak: "I fought but could not help it. It was for home or against home. I fought for this cabin."

Lincoln, who was as much the pioneer type as Grandpa Frazee, was as representative of America and Americanism as Andrew Jackson. Lindsay pointed out that "Lincoln was elected as a far western man," and he stated that Sangamon County in the middle of the century was "Rail Splitters" country—"and not a mere Middle West." Lindsay never disassociated the log cabin from Lincoln. And having written in one place, "Lincoln is finally, to me, a typical Virginia man," he said elsewhere: "I have always considered Abraham Lincoln essentially a Southerner and a Jeffersonian and liberal Protestant."

Lindsay did not share Masters' opinion that John Brown was a foolish "busybody"; much less did he regard John Wilkes

Booth as a "patriot." Quite the opposite, he was so incensed against Booth that he had him roasted in Hell:

> When John Wilkes Booth shot Lincoln
> the good,
> He hid himself in a deep Potomac Wood,
> But the devil came and got him and dragged
> him below.
>
> "A Curse for the Saxophone"

And, far from considering Calhoun, the champion of "states rights," a Southern patriot, Lindsay has Andrew Jackson hanging him because he offends as a Secessionist.

Lincoln, "a real poet," not only appears in Lindsay's "Litany of Heroes," but also figures as a leading character in his mythology of folk heroes. In his *Village Magazine* Lindsay drew a picture of Lincoln's home with angels swinging censers over it. He crowned this by drawing a second illustration of Lincoln's monument with angels swinging censers over it. His reverence for Lincoln exceeded his worship of Jefferson:

> The buildings associated with Linclon stand for the most precious tradition in America. The greatest use of these buildings is in giving our citizens spirit pictures of the future, when the slaves of special tyrannies of the twentieth century shall be set free. These citizens feel assured that Springfield is going to be the place where arrogant idleness and the caste system, and the wicked notions that go with them are abolished.

Only the term "idolatry," describes Lindsay's attitude to Lincoln. It might be an exaggeration to say that he attributed to Lincoln Messianic qualities, but Lindsay did regard him as superhuman. In the fantasy of *Lincoln in India*, Lindsay said of him: "He is standing this hour on the banks of the Ganges at Benares." It is hardly surprising that one of his finest poems was inspired by Lincoln: "Abraham Lincoln Walks at Midnight." In this poem Lindsay not only deifies the dead leader, but also gives unrestrained expression to his own pacifism and his love for the common man:

. . . .
Too many peasants fight, they know not why.
Too many homesteads in black terror weep.

The sins of all the war lords burn his heart.
He sees the dreadnaughts scouring every main.
He carries on his shawl-wrapped shoulders now
The bitterness the folly and the pain.

He cannot rest until a spirit-dawn
Shall come;—the shining hope of Europe free:
The league of sober folk, the Workers' Earth,
Bringing long peace to Cornland, Alp and Sea. . . .

Theodore Roosevelt also appears in Lindsay's "Litany of Heroes"; he is honored because he chained "King Mammon in the donjon-keep." It is for Roosevelt's sake that N. M. Naylor, the "Good Printer," receives his meed of praise, for it was Naylor who made "clear Roosevelt's marvellous shout." The poem, "In Which Roosevelt Is Compared to Saul," first published in 1913, Lindsay published again on Theodore Roosevelt's death. He entitled another poem, "Hail To the Sons of Roosevelt," and a third, long poem, which he wrote "for the Illinois State Teachers' Association," he had "printed as a broadside, read, and distributed the same day (April 4, 1929)," and he titled it simply "Roosevelt."

Comparing Roosevelt with the "stuffed prophets," he claimed that Roosevelt's "sins were better than their sweetest goodness." He averred passionately that "money" hated Roosevelt:

. . . .
They talk of "dollars" and "dollars"
and "dollars"
And "dollars" and "dollars," and hate
his clean soul.

96

Oh money, money—that *never* can think,
Money, money, that *never* can rule.
Always an anarchist, always an idiot.

In this condemnation of money, Lindsay's "romantic" theory
of history became one with Masters' "money" theory. Lindsay
hated "money" which was representative of trusts and banks,
a strictly Populist hatred, with the same intensity as Masters.
Yet, unlike Masters, where money was concerned, Lindsay
made every effort to be honest with himself, and he admitted
his own temptations and self-deceit:

> Let me declare that I love money. At work in the city
> I have the usual human feeling that I am not getting all
> the cash my work deserves. I am just as deferential as
> you, good reader, to people of wealth especially if they
> have used their leisure to acquire culture. I have the usual
> shrinking from the man whose father did not obtain for
> him early in life an environment of porcelain bath tub
> and full dinner pail. I realize that this bulletin is a hot
> house production, the conservatory was built with other
> men's dollars. In my usual speeches as a Y.M.C.A. man,
> an Anti-Saloon man and a Disciple of Christ, I am apt to
> say the things that don't disturb business. But on the
> road I eat of the Perilous Flower and preach the sermon
> for strangers.

That Lindsay's hostility to money is Populist-conditioned is
evident in both his life and writings, and his short symbolic
poem, "Hieroglyphic of the Soul of a Spider," is but one of
the many expressions he gave to his attitude. A second poem
revelatory of this hostility is "Factory Windows Are Always
Broken," broken, by "the bitter, snarling, derisive stone." Em-
ploying metaphor, Lindsay claimed that he did not believe in
"class war," but in the "war of the mountain and the desert
with the town." He stated: "Only the deserts of America can
break the business hardened skulls of the east."

97

Lindsay's own estimate of himself was that he was a radical, and although describing the radicals as "shabby hysterical cats," he wrote: "I had rather be with the cats than the compromisers."[20] Since Populism was dying as an identifiable movement during the period that Lindsay was reaching his maturity and there was no Populist organization which could claim his allegiance, it was natural and logical that Lindsay should become a Socialist. Herein his enthusiasm for religion and his passion for politics merged: "I believe in Christ the Socialist, the Beautiful, the personal saviour from sin, the Singing Immanuel."

Lindsay for a time regarded himself as an undiluted Socialist, and he had, in fact, a place for Socialism in his personal crusade:

> The New State House stands, in this book as the representative of that handful of legislators, constantly growing in influence, who, for many sessions in the future are destined to a triumphant battle for a Socialist Illinois.

The great emotions that politics aroused in Lindsay resulted in occasional poems written in a sudden burst of feeling and inspiration. This was not Lindsay's normal manner of writing, for unlike Masters, he was an "indefatigable worker." Lindsay himself testified: "I rewrite my poems fifty times as a matter of course,"[21] and he said of a poem on which he was working: "I have been over it two and a half times and hope to go over it seventeen and a half times more."[22]

But when Lindsay learned, on the evening of March 1, 1911, that "the United States Senate had declared the election of William Booth good and valid, by a vote of forty-six to forty, he sat down and wrote down two poems of triumph, one of which, "To Reformers in Despair," was printed the following morning in *The Illinois State Register*. The second he entitled, "Why I Voted the Socialist Ticket." It was poems of this nature which caused Alfred Kreymborg to write: "Lindsay went straight to the masses, like a socialistic orator, and harangued the mob from metaphoric soap boxes."

Populism, as has been mentioned, identified itself with democratic movements in other countries. At variance with this aspect was the pronounced xenophobia found in Masters and in many "isolationist" Middle-Westerners. Lindsay, however, was a cosmopolitan. Thus when the Russian Revolution shocked the world in 1917, Lindsay hailed the end of Tsarism with the same enthusiasm that the weakening of feudalism in Japan had been hailed in *Tom Watson's Magazine*. For him the Russian Revolution meant the possible emancipation of the oppressed. He had developed from a "Jane Addams and Byran follower to a Kerensky follower," but when the Kerensky government failed and was succeeded by that of the Bolsheviks, Lindsay was unable to embrace Marxism:

> I agree with [Waldo] Frank absolutely in regard to Lincoln and Mark Twain, and I fancy in little else. The disguised Marxism that is evidently back of his book, gives me the nausea and the pain from a literary standpoint.[23]

There is considerable significance in Lindsay's rejection of Marxism, and, ultimately in his rejection of Socialism. During the World War I period, Lindsay became an avowed internationalist, but the internationalism inherent in Communist ideology did not persuade him to regard the Bolshevik regime in Russia with any favor. His hostility toward Communism was not inconsistent even though Communism had some things in common with Lindsay's Populism. Ideally, the two political theories agreed in their avowed intention to establish a classless society, in their antagonism to economic exploitation, and in the "withering away of the State."

In spite of these points of agreement, there were issues between Communism and Lindsay's Populism which, for him, were decisive. Chief among these was Lindsay's "New Localism": His greatest objection to Marxism internationalism was that it tried to unify by destroying boundaries. Thus there would be no line between Indiana and Illinois.

Supplementing this objection was Lindsay's pacifism, to which Lindsay later devoted all of section IX in his *Collected Poems*. The poem, "A Curse for Kings," stated his belief that wars were caused by insane European monarchs, and "The Unpardonable Sin" was to "send rapine in the name of Christ." "To Jane Addams At the Hague" was an exhortation that she "Stand now for peace (though anger breaks your heart)." "Who Knows" stated the idea that the repercussion of European Wars go far "Till every far off homestead goes insane." "Shantung," "Abraham Lincoln Walks at Midnight," "Above the Battle Front," and other poems expressed similar sentiments. So strong was Lindsay's anti-militarism, in fact, that he managed to inject the feeling into such unlikely subjects as a contemporaneous review of a William S. Hart "cowboy" picture: "Glory Hole was as pure as Cromwell's Parliament after Pride's Purge, or Europe will be after Prussian Militarism is annihilated." It was hardly surprising that Lindsay found himself out of sympathy with Communism, which made the use of force a primary instrument of policy.

When Woodrow Wilson involved the United States in the Great European War, Lindsay did much soul-searching. He wrote:

> My heart is very sad tonight about the war. I have not the heart to challenge Wilson. I voted for him and cannot regret it—yet Jane Addam's dauntless fight for peace goes home to my soul. I feel with her—and with him—and am all torn inside.

In attempting to analyze his pacifist attitude toward World War I, which was in conflict with the slogans of saving the world for democracy, Lindsay wondered whether he was "self-deceived." He began to doubt his pacifism and went so far as to declare that he would have been in the ranks if his literary work "had not seemed my first duty." It was his hope that out of the war would come a World Government and that Wilson would be its first President. Of Wilson he wrote: "Though he lets Debs go to jail, yet I am for him, for he is radical by comparison with the Mikado and the Kaiser"; and in his "Litany of Heroes," Lindsay compared Wilson to Socrates.

Lindsay's enthusiasm for Wilson may also have been bolstered by the fact that Wilson had appointed William Jennings Bryan, Secretary of State, (Bryan's reward for helping Wilson to secure the Presidential nomination), an appointment very pleasing to Lindsay and like-minded Middle-Western agrarians.

Wilson's "more" government did not persuade Lindsay to turn against Wilson, but criticism of Wilson and America, by such professional German propagandists as George Sylvester Viereck, destroyed his faith in Socialism. He now saw Socialism as an alien Germanic creed, which had no place in a Jeffersonian America. Lindsay felt so strongly about the matter that he made a public announcement, in *Dial*, of his renunciation.

> The very mention of the Revolutionary Fathers has become a suspicious matter nowadays, simply because professional pro-Kaiserites like Viereck used them to suggest we should hate England. . . . I have reached the point where as a formerly avowed voter of the Socialist ticket in America, the very mention of the Socialist party gives me a nausea almost physical. The St. Louis Platform has cured me for all time, I presume, of all German importations of this sort.
> "A Word of Advice about Policy"

Lindsay maintained that the letters of Jefferson had laid down the true course for the American people. He saw the post-World War I period as a world reconstruction period following upon the American Revolutionary War and out of which would come "A Constitution of the World." The Federalist papers, he wrote

> have far more for us this hour than any platform written for any breed of Marxism. . . .

101

The American system as it stands, ruthlessly applied, would eliminate classes, and we would have no class war, nor anything that could be misdescribed. All America would be upper middle world, if the total of our private citizens used the pick and shovel as the drafted men do in camp and used the ballot in the same way.

Lindsay did not see the class war in the same stark and uncompromising terms as did the Communists. For him, nothing more was needed to abolish the class war than the people's love for doing their own work:

> Any American who pushes his own lawn mower abolishes the class war, and the majority of them, Democrats or Republicans, do push their own lawn mowers, and hate Kings and Multimillionaires, and expect to abolish Kings and Multimillionaires.

Thus Lindsay's traditional spirit, so decisive for the Populist, with its pride of place, its yearnings for a past which contained the "ideal America" and the "American way of life," was so fundamental that it proved conclusive in Lindsay's evaluations of immediate issues such as Socialism and Communism.

CHAPTER VI

VACHEL LINDSAY

Literary Heroes and Agrarian Prototypes

Lindsay's literary forebears, his agrarian prototypes and his ideal American village were very similar to those of Masters. *Huckleberry Finn* and *Tom Sawyer* were woven into the fabric of Lindsay's ideal, but in his case the weave was much tighter than it was in Masters'. *Tom Sawyer* exercised such a fascination for Lindsay that he read it each year, from his eighth to his fifteenth year. Moreover, and significantly, the setting for his reading was Grandfather Frazee's farm in Indiana. The book, it seems, was a prize, for Lindsay "took turns in reading it and rereading it."[24] Tom Sawyer's "innocent America we lived in then," was very much like Rush County, Indiana.

Lindsay recalled that *Tom Sawyer* and *Huckleberry Finn* were forbidden, till it was discovered that to give those two books to the young was one way of keeping them quiet. For Lindsay, Mark Twain was not limited to his boyhood: "The authority of Mark Twain's personality grows through the years." Lindsay saw Mark Twain as "an old Southern colonel disguised as a humorist," and he contended that Twain had chivalry, describing his worship of Joan of Arc as magnificent. Finally, Mark Twain's language was bonafide American. In support of this claim, Lindsay informed his readers that "Mark Twain writes Virginia with *r*," and made the statement that

103

the langauge of Virginia constituted the *real* American language.

Lindsay wrote a triad of poems on Mark Twain, which he entitled respectively, "The Raft," "When the Mississippi Flowed in Indiana," and "Mark Twain and Joan of Arc." In these poems Lindsay recreated the river world of Huckleberry Finn, which symbolizes the world of youthful America, as a wonderful and courageous world.

Walt Whitman was another of Lindsay's forebears and their affinity is evident in such lines as:

> I am the pioneer
> Voice of Democracy
> I am the gutter dream
> I am the golden dream.

Such a style and sentiment caused Lindsay to be compared with Whitman and to be regarded as a follower of Whitman. But Lindsay soon made it evident that "he did not care for Whitman, whom he is so often told he resembles." Lindsay, in fact, ultimately reacted to Whitman much as Masters had reacted to Bryan: "But I disposed of Whitman as a personal hero, without quoting St. Paul, yet maintaining precisely the Pauline standard of behavior." [25]

Contrary to his usual forbearance, Lindsay seized several opportunities to attack Whitman. In one letter he castigated Whitman, who "never saw the America I have seen and loved," saying of him:

> Walt Whitman in his wildest dreams was only a pretended troubadour. He sat still in cafes. Never such a troubadour as Bryan or a thousand Chautauqua men.

Lindsay's disaffection with Whitman seems to have had multiple reasons. Lindsay found "no confession in Whitman"; he also found Whitman, like Washington, tainted with "the grand style." Whitman, both as a man and a poet, had no chivalry. Lindsay predicted that Whitman would probably be

104

"separated from democracy as Milton and Michael Angelo are."

In view of this hostility, it is curious that Whitman's name was allowed to remain in Lindsay's "Litany of the Heroes" as the pupil of "shining Emerson." Lindsay had condemned Whitman some years before his *Collected Poems*, published in 1923. The inconsistency was carried a step further when Lindsay, without any necessity to do so, used a review of an anthology as an excuse to launch one of his bitterest attacks:

> While we are reading it, it delivers us from Whitman, thank God! If you only want American poetry, I suggest that you forget Whitman a moment, and read *Yanks*. It contains an invisible writing which appears on the fourth reading, and which was never in Whitman, even on the tenth reading.

A year later, he was once again tilting at Whitman, Lindsay stated:

> I have said for years that if almost everything that was said in praise of Whitman was rewritten with the name of Johnny Appleseed and Abraham Lincoln substituted, it would be much truer, in the eyes of America.[26]

Lindsay was unable to deny that Sandburg owed a direct debt to Whitman, but he offset the acknowledgment by reminding his readers that Sandburg was "something more than a Whitmanite."

In addition to Twain and Whitman, Lindsay had been saturated with James Whitcomb Riley:

> A dearly loved aunt of mine sent me one book of Riley's poems every year, on Christmas, from the time I was eight years old till I grew up. For years and years I had a Riley education and gloried in it.

The Riley education was so embedded in Lindsay that he was incapable of an objective estimate of Riley's works. Thus Lindsay, as unobjective as Masters, could express an opinion which no detached critic could subscribe to:

> Poe might die, but we would suddenly find Riley much more alive . . . Riley was never witty and flip. He was either deeply and classically humorous or a failure.[27]

This intense provincialism of Lindsay not only resulted on occasion in curious estimates of literary merit in others, but sometimes led him into absurdities. He seriously considered writing

> a long epic on the *American Turkey Gobbler*. I have all data, if I can make him gobble. I think the turkey is more wonderful and beautiful than the (griffin), and handsome, but people only eat him. I am dreaming of turkey fanciers, who breed him for his beauty like the peacock. And he has a more substantial cry.[28]

John Chapman, popularly known as Johnny Appleseed, was Lindsay's prototype of the sweet humanitarian agrarian, and also a liberal source of inspiration. Lindsay made a study of Johnny Appleseed's itinerary: "(He) did not get as far west as Illinois; but he tramped toward it, straight West from the Boston region," and although he did not duplicate this itinerary in his own tramping, he may well have fancied himself a Johnny Appleseed planting beauty in men's souls.

The number of poems that Lindsay wrote about Johnny Appleseed demonstrate that John Chapman played an important part in Lindsay's thinking. In fact, many parallels between Lindsay and Chapman can be observed in "Johnny Appleseed's Life of the Mind," "Johnny Appleseed's Hymn to the Sun," "Johnny Appleseed's Ship Comes In," "Johnny Appleseed Speaks of the Apple-Blossom Amaranth that Will Come to This City," "Johnny Appleseed's Wife from the Palace of Eve," and "How Johnny Appleseed Walked Alone in the Jungles of Heaven." In addition to these poems Lindsay wrote a triad of poems which he called "In Praise of Johnny Appleseed."

106

This tendency to glorify certain individuals to the proportion of legend is typical of the intense nationalism of which Lindsay is so excellent a representative. This is an element in the obsession of which George Orwell has said: "As nearly as possible, no nationalist ever thinks, talks, or writes about anything except the superiority of his own power unit."

This obsession is not necessarily stable, and in his attitude to his contemporary literary heroes, Lindsay's constancy suffered noticeably, perhaps because the living may betray an ideal, whereas the dead cannot. Lindsay confessed:

> My own highly personal list of living American wise men changes every year a bit. Right now it is headed by William Allen White, Edgar Lee Masters, Robert Frost and Carl Sandburg.

Lindsay's Crusade

Lindsay's treks provided him with a first-hand knowledge of the small American town. On his return to Springfield in 1908, Lindsay began his "war with Springfield respectability, with the stereotyped United States in general." This, Lindsay averred, was the war which the artist had to wage "till death," although he did not regard it as a tragedy, "but (as) akin to one hundred Gilbert and Sullivan Operas."

Lindsay, in this early period, had "iron in his soul," but eventually, he was to become "hysterical through going it alone."[29] Nevertheless, the years 1908-12 constitute the period when his pamphlets "began to fly in Springfield." He recorded that he was straightway dropped from the rolls of the Y.M.C.A. and the Anti-Saloon League, but he harbored no ill-feelings, contenting himself with the explanation that: "No Y.M.C.A. or Anti-Saloon League worker likes an Art Student, even if he floods the town, [sic] gratis with tracts."

Lindsay was by no means dismayed because he was poor, unknown, and as he himself said, regarded as "queer." He announced that it was his intention to make Civics "as much

107

a religion, as healing is a religion in Christian Science, or Undertaking was a religion in Egypt,"[30] and he had both a philosophy of propaganda and a means to conduct his political evangelism. In 1914, after he had achieved some recognition, he wrote to Jessie B. Rittenhouse:

> Bid the poets go forth to conquer the 90 Million Americans. They are singing on an island to one another, while the people perish. I do not think there need be much change in the character of the songs—as the things sung about—it is a question of the poet's personal lives—a question of their laying hold of the people as the Preachers and Priests and Politicians do, and, in Europe, the Military Aristocracy. In our land the Progressives are for the present demoralized, the Socialists are put out of countenance by the war—at least as internationalists—it remains for the Poetic Oligarchy to dominate. The people are waiting. Let us climb on the soapboxes and call them to us with a cheerful call, or solemn call, according to our songs.
>
> Certainly if the Soldiers claim Europe, we Poets have a right to claim America.[31]

When this crusading zeal made itself felt in Lindsay it did so dominatively. Evidence is found in the fact that he published his tracts at his own expense and distributed them either without payment of any kind or merely on payment of postage. A letter to his printer reveals a man who marched to his own drumbeat, independent of the commercial publishers who had rejected his early work:

> My Dear Storey:
>
> Please print the first thousand for me of the Village Parade and Gospel of Beauty. Use the words enclosed (sic) for the Gospel. I have reasonable assurances of wages on the ranches here the next few weeks and want

the matter ready as soon as work is over. I will take your cheapest terms . . .[32]

This willingness to sacrifice his all for a poetic programme designed to change Springfield and America was no temporary undertaking. In a letter to Conrad Aiken he recalled:

I have put into circulation for the last fifteen years pamphlets of pen-and-ink drawings, at my own expense. Every time I put my entire bank account into the venture and went into debt from one year to three in the enterprise.

Lindsay did not hesitate to enlist the aid of anyone who revealed sympathy for his cause and who might help in spreading his gospel. A letter to a Mrs. May Lamberton Becker is altogether characteristic:

Thank you indeed for your interest in my work. I send you an envelope of my goods under separate cover. Anyone is welcome to this. Of course if you are talking to large groups of people I do not insist that you mention it. But the few in any town who talk to you afterwards and really care—are welcome. Six cents in stamps if they want to.[33]

Lindsay's first salvo against the burghers of Springfield was contained in *War Bulletin No. 1*, which, dated July 19, 1909, sold for five cents. In explaining why he selected such a title Lindsay said:

I have spent a great part of my years fighting a soul battle for absolute liberty, for freedom from obligation, ease of conscience, independence of commercialism.

His independence was complete, for he was not only free of the restrictions he might feel necessary in order to please publishers, but he was also free of the need to please his readers:

The things that go into the War Bulletin please me only, to the Devil with you, Average reader. To Gehenna with your stupidity, your bigotry, your conservatism, your cheapness and impatience.

His first Bulletin ended with a threat to attack "Conventional Christianity as it is practiced in the remote and nefarious village of Morristown, New Jersey, the wealthiest little burg in the United States."

War Bulletin No. 2 followed on August 4, 1909, and was succeeded by *War Bulletin No. 3* only three weeks later, on August 30, 1909. With the third issue the five cents charge was suspended, for henceforth the Bulletins were to be

> as free as butter in a hospitable house. He who helps to pass the fire of the Bulletins from mind to mind, has done the greatest possible to do for the publisher thereof.

War Bulletin No. 4 carried the subtitle, *The Tramp's Excuse,* and in it appeared Lindsay's "Map of the Universe" of which he said: "This Map is One Beginning of The Golden Book of Springfield."

Lindsay's "Map of the Universe," in conjunction with his "The Village Improvement Parade," is of importance, according to him, in understanding his message. Described by Lindsay as a "hieroglyphic drawing," its center of interest is an area called "the throne mountains," which rest in billowing clouds called "the jungles of heaven." The Miltonic and Blakean influences seem to predominate. "The Village Improvement Parade" is both a stylized drawing of young men and women bearing banners with slogans on them and a poem.

Pictorial propaganda seems to have ranked as equal in Lindsay's mind to poetic propaganda. Even as late as the publication of his *Complete Poems* he was writing:

> I have been an art student all my life, in the strictest sense of the word. I have been so exclusively an art student, I am still surprised to be called a writer.

Lindsay used *War Bulletin No. 4* as the basis of a book foreshadowing the Millennium in Springfield, but he destroyed it before publication because "it seemed to provoke such amazing wrath." Nevertheless, Lindsay was incapable of destroying anything—in one way or another everything he created was always reproduced. This was the case with *War Bulletin No. 4*, which was reborn as *The Golden Book of Springfield*.

War Bulletin No. 5 appeared in the Thanksgiving season of 1909, and in it Lindsay celebrated the naturalization of Paul Reps, a Russian laborer. This issue also lauded the contributions to America of such minorities as the Italians, the Lithuanians, and the Jews. He exhorted foreigners not to waste their precious youth in industry on the pleas that America is already too rich and needs not material progress, but "lacks most those things that come to idle men."

In this Bulletin, too, Lindsay's fancy took wild flight, and he pleaded an immaterialism that seems extravagant for the audience to which it was addressed:

> Oh farmers, so jealous of your grain, give all your time to fields of clouds and air. There the harvests are truly plenteous and the laborers few. The man with a house painted and fields in order is in danger of hell fire.

For the Christmas season of 1909 Lindsay published his *The Sangamon County Peace Advocate, No. 1*. This brochure, which, like the War Bulletins, he published at his own expense, contains nine poems, two of which, "Springfield Magical" and "Someday Our Town Will Grow Old" are important because they are part of the beginning of Lindsay's "New Localism." "Springfield Magical" expresses the idea of the universality of Springfield:

> In this, the City of Discontent
> Sometimes there comes a whisper from the grass:—
> Romance, Romance—is here. No Hindu town
> Is quite so strange. No citadel of grass

By Sinbad found, held half such love and hate.
No picture palace in a picture book,
Such webs of friendship, beauty, greed and fate.

The War Bulletins were followed by what Lindsay called *The Village Magazine*, which was a "portfolio" of his poems, articles, drawings from his art student and later days, and his War Bulletins. *The Village Magazine* was not to be a monthly magazine but a "decade" and a "destiny" magazine. It was reissued in 1920 and in 1925, and Lindsay looked forward to a 1930 issue. The title of the magazine has considerable Populist significance, for the Village is Lindsay's essential message. He preached the distinctive Populist theory that American cities are dead, while villages are the "fortunate islands in the wild seas of commerce." It is these same villages which in rare moments, so Lindsay claimed, brought to him "the elusive charm of the dead and the immortal Hellas." An editorial appears on behalf of the "wise man in the metropolis concerning the humble agricultural village in Central Illinois." Another editorial appears "for the art student who has returned to the village," whether from Chicago, New York, London, Paris or Berlin. Its text is: "If you have any cherished beauty undertake it where you are. You will find no better place in all America." A poem appears, "The Illinois Village," in which "The railroad is a thing disowned. The city but a field of weeds." For those "Who weep that liberty must die" Lindsay's cure is the simple one of turning to "the little prairie towns."

In *The Village Magazine* appeared the pronunciamento that a "blacksmith aristocracy" is the permanent ideal of the American nation. Lindsay was convinced that this aristocracy was "thoroughly established" by the founders of the Constitution, though "modern mammonites and Marxians rave at it in vain."

The Golden Book of Springfield

In 1915, Lindsay resolved to "block in" *The Golden Book of Springfield*, hoping that the book would have a definite

112

effect on the history of Springfield; his aim being to convert at least five out of every hundred readers of his book into rabid followers. As his correspondence with Louis Untermeyer reveals, once he started on the work it became an obsession. As late as 1920 Lindsay wrote: "I have driven harder and longer on this work than on anything I have ever done in my life."[34]

The Springfield that Lindsay loved had much in common with the New Salem and Petersburg of Masters. It was a place where "fire laddies and their sweethearts of an hour" jammed the local Arsenal for a town dance; where, in celebration of "peace," the townspeople held a parade which continued until midnight, a parade in which Lindsay took part most of the time. It was a place where, conveniently for Lindsay, some new preacher swooped down and denounced liquor with such eloquence that the leaders of the "wets" were converted and the wet petition was thrown into the wastebasket. "Everybody gets married, and oh, the lovely babies that ensue."

In the *Golden Book* Lindsay's mystique reached its utmost limits. Here he envisioned his ideal of a world government and foresaw it established by the year 2018. Three flags symbolize the spirit of this united world: "that of the town, that of the International Government, and above these, the Star Spangled Banner."

This world of the twenty-first century was to be as agrarian as Kansas and as lacking in industries as Springfield. It never occurred to Lindsay that without the modern techniques of production and communication—the products of industrialism —such a world, even had it been achieved, would have fallen into disunity through isolation, lack of information, and the paucity of contacts. Nor did Lindsay's Populist nationalism allow him to so much as suspect that there might exist large numbers of people who were metropolitan by inclination. Because the Middle West gave him strength and inspiration, he made the large assumption that it would have the same effect on all the people of the world. He claimed that the people inhabiting his twenty-first century Utopia would "pride them-

113

selves in being more democratic, and not parading their ancestry."

The extent to which Lindsay was bemused by literary Populists of his own power unit is evident in the fact that he had parks in his Utopia named after Edgar Lee Masters and Carl Sandburg. It is hardly surprising that, to an outsider, Lindsay's nationalism, because it was so intensely provincial and unknown, proved bewildering. An English reviewer confessed that, in reading *The Golden Book of Springfield*, he had been through "a real, if baffling experience."

This intense nationalism, although more marked in the last two hundred years, has appeared from time to time throughout the history of civilization. Even the Greeks, so comprehensive in their thinking, dismissed all non-Greeks as barbarians, while a people as rational and philosophical as the Germans embraced a nationalism of German blood and German soil which took on the aspects of pagan mysticism. Lindsay's nationalism was centered in Springfield, and, unlike Masters' nationalism, it was not exclusive. Like the Roman leaders, Lindsay was eager to extend the blessings of his power unit to the whole of mankind.

Conclusion

The years 1908-1912, before he achieved a national reputation with his *General Booth* poem, constitute the period of which Lindsay was most proud, and in which he made his most characteristic utterance. "Springfield," he wrote

> is still a place of lifetime intimates who regret everything
> I have ever done . . . and everything up to October 1912.
> They are sure I pretend to have been born 1912, and so
> ignore all my painful past.

Adverse critics failed to understand him, and while one complained that Lindsay "spent fifteen years of his life in hieroglyphic nonsense," another, having remarked on "the thinness and poverty of his impressions," added with some indignation: "A few flowers among the railroad track, plenty of queer people, wheat interminably. . . ." To these and others, Lindsay retorted:

> Critics are still instructing me in elementary matters they would find summarized in the bulletins if they went on the hunt. I, too, have been instructive (sarcasm).

After 1912, having made his name nationally famous, Lindsay, spent most of his remaining twenty years as a vagabond poet, lecturer and observer. This role was by no means displeasing to Lindsay, for in it he was actively pursuing what he described as his "greatest desire," which was that "his entire message, his rounded work, should reach the people." To this end, he adopted the role of the missionary, going to the people and descending to their level by addressing them in a language he felt they could understand. Lindsay rationalized the vulgarization of his work thus:

> The American people hate and abhor poetry. I am inventing a sort of ragtime manner that deceives them into thinking they are at a vaudeville show, and yet I try to keep it to a real art.

The vulgarization of diction was part of the agrarian writers' program for a genuinely democratic art. The language of the man on the farm and the man on the street was to be used, and this was the language used by Lindsay, who fortunately deferred to the opinion of Susan E. Wilcox: "Week after week for six months I read the verse till she was sure it was clear, grammatical and reasonable."

Allied to the diction of the "common man" were what Harriet Monroe has described as "the seductions of the moment," the subjects with popular appeal, "Subjects like Mark Twain, prairies and buffaloes, Kerensky, Niagara, which move us whether the poet enriches them or not." Although Lindsay was well aware that a "really trained man," as he called the artist, had very little in common with the man on the street, he could

115

not resist the temptation to win the rapport of his audience. Carl Van Doren has offered an explanation for this:

> The crusader cannot be a connoisseur. He must meet the masses of men something like half-way. Nor can it be merely in the matter of language that he meets them. He must share as well a fair number of their enthusiasms and antipathies. He must have gusto, temper, rhetoric; must apply them to topics which are not too much refined by nice distinctions.

Lindsay nourished the belief that there must be a close personal relationship between the poet and his hearers. His methods of trading his rhymes for bread, even though at times "housewives sicked their dogs on him," and his handing out of his pamphlets and broadsides gratuitously, established the most intimate relationship possible between the poet and his hearers. At the same time, Lindsay was trying to express the Middle West, which he was persuaded could be "expressed," despite the fact that there were those who claimed that "the Middle West is still very much a place and very little a philosophy or an emotion."

When Lindsay wrote of "the West," or of the prairie, of Kansas, of the pioneer, and of the people, he adopted what Carl Van Doren has called "the windy lingo of the booster," the same language used by the railroads in their drive for settlers and by local chambers of commerce in their competition for population and business. Lindsay was convinced that this area had "inspirational vitality" and he was inordinately proud that the "prairie country was the West, 'Wild and Woolly,' where *most anything* might happen."

In the same way that Masters had urged the people to visit Petersburg, Lindsay urged his audiences to visit Springfield and, if possible, the whole West. He wrote to Louis Untermeyer:

> . . . make an ample visit to this town, sometime soon. We will spend the morning reading Moon Calf. We will spend

the rest of the day proving or disproving it on the streets of Springfield. We will spend the next morning reading Mitch Miller. We will spend the rest of the day proving or disproving it on the streets of Springfield. . . .[35]

Lindsay invited Stephen Graham, one of his biographers, "to seek with him the source of American spirit in the mountains of the West," and Graham, who tramped the West with him, observed that "Vachel indulged his passion for the West and all that the West means to an American."

It was Lindsay's desire that the West should remain unchanged; he pleaded: "Let it remain the free young West, yet become a land where sacred rivers have place."

The huge expanse of prairie that made up the Middle West assumed a mystic significance for Lindsay, and the prairie is often present, either overtly expressed or more covertly as background, in such poems of Lindsay's as "The Ghosts of Buffaloes," "The Bronco that Would Not Be Broken," "The Santa Fe Trail," and "The Cornfield." The poem, "Prairie Battlements," appropriately dedicated to Edgar Lee Masters, begins:

Here upon the prairie
Is our ancestral hall.
Agate is the dome,
Cornelian the wall.

For Masters, as we have seen, the state of Illinois represented his ideal American State, and for Lindsay Kansas fulfilled the same role. He becomes rapturous when he describes it:

Kansas, the Ideal American Community,
Kansas, nearer than any other to the kind
of a land our fathers took for granted,
Kansas practically free from cities and
industrialism, the real last refuge of
the Constitution.

117

When he celebrated Kansas in his poem, "The Santa Fe Trail," he hailed it as place of refreshment and restoration:

> Ho for Kansas, land that restores us
> When houses choke us, and great books
> bore us.

Several critics have remarked on Lindsay's identification of himself with Kansas, chief among them being William Dean Howells, who stated: "Here is no shredding of prose, but much of oaten stop and pastoral song, such as rises amid the hum of the Kansas harvest fields. . . ." Albert Edmund Trombly wrote: "The never-ending expanse of the Kansas wheat fields has entered into his soul," and Fred Lewis Pattee with great discernment pointed out: "His apostrophe to the State reveals the meaning of his later chantings."

Here we encounter Lindsay's unmistakable message. His ideal America was an agricultural kingdom as open and fertile as Kansas, punctuated with villages and hamlets which were replicas of Springfield. It was against this background, he believed, where men gave attention to the soil, and where they were free of the corruptions and confinements of the city, that the people would find salvation. It is not surprising that he was referred to as a "corn-fed poetic chick" and as a man from "corny regions," but Lindsay accepted such epithets as adulatory, and he deliberately used such terms in a commendatory sense: "When I plan the future of some hypothetical poet west of the Mississippi, I insist that he be corn-fed and ramping, and write for the farmers, and go shouting along. . . ."

It is the failure to appreciate the Populistic paradox of Jeffersonian liberalism and Jacksonian despotism of "the people," which caused many critics to stray in their evaluation of Lindsay's message. This was the case even with Louis Untermeyer, who, though well equipped to assess Lindsay's aims and intentions, failed to detect logic in Lindsay's thinking and could make no sense of his America:

> His was a motley America . . . Lindsay saw these dis-
> united States finally united by a congress or a conjunction

of pioneers and baseball players, Presidents and movie queens.

It is precisely this type of criticism, which leaves out of account Lindsay's fanatical nationalism, his basic tolerance of everything he regarded as essentially American, that has made Lindsay seem naïve and irrational.

Lindsay's crusade against the evergrowing philistinism of America never became bitter or misanthropic. America was his life-long blind spot, as Harriet Monroe has noted:

> It is hardly necessary, perhaps, to mention Mr. Lindsay's loyalty to the people of his place and hour or the training in sympathy with their aims and ideals which he has achieved through vagabondish wanderings in the Middle West.

There is considerable significance in the fact that, unlike many of the literary expatriates who left America because they hated or disliked the United States, Lindsay along with his compeers, Masters and Sandburg, choose to stay at home. And the significance is enhanced when it is known that, while in England, Lindsay spent his time writing about Springfield.

Springfield was so deep in Lindsay's blood and bones that he repeatedly vowed to return there "and stay forevermore," and Jessie B. Rittenhouse has observed: "No passion more enduring than that which Vachel Lindsay felt for his boyhood could be conceived." And the ultimate nature of Springfield is seen in the fact that "He was happier when he pleased Springfield than when the world acclaimed him." Finally, just as Masters, in his old age, had returned to give a speech on the steps of the Petersburg courthouse, similarly Lindsay's last public reading was given in a Springfield church a week before his death.

In sum, Vachel Lindsay, like Masters, was a thoroughgoing Middle-Western agrarian reformer. Like Masters he could criticize, but he was unable to offer little in the way of constructive suggestion. In this he reflected not so much his deficiencies in the realm of political and economic analysis as the preju-

119

dices of his agrarian milieu. He was sure that industrialism and the East offered no acceptable alternative to a Jeffersonian America. Ascetic by nature, he envisioned his Springfield foregoing the advances of technology, and remaining a small Athens in the heart of the prairie.

Lindsay shared Masters' belief in the cult of the pioneer and of the farmer; he also held Masters' opinion that the Americans who followed were a lesser breed. However, an important difference between the two men, apart from their opposed attitudes to Lincoln, was in temperament; Masters was congenitally pessimistic, Lindsay was optimistic. Lindsay was sure that the Jeffersonian America in which he believed would come, although, like so many other idealists and Utopians, he had no faith that his own generation would establish it. This faith in the human being of the future was not matched by faith in his contemporaries, for in one of his last poems, published posthumously, he heaped on them a scorn reminiscent of Masters:

> Oh, shame upon you, sons of men
> You cannot laugh nor weep
> Till you have lost the coin of men.
> And then have drunken deep.
> "A Song During Business Depression"

Lindsay was representative of the agricultural America which the post-Civil War industrialism had replaced. As V. F. Calverton phrased it:

> When Vachel Lindsay, at the age of fifty-two, put an end to his life by swallowing lysol, it was more than a man who died. It was an age as well as an individual expiring in his last words: 'They tried to get me; I got them first.'

In spite of Lindsay's appeal to the man on the farm and on the street, his background was that of the sophisticate. As he pointed out, he had trod the corridors of the Metropolitan Museum for eighteen years. In his poetry he never pretended

120

to be an "uncouth swain," a country Burns. He knew Greek models, and his rhymes have been called "some of the most skillful in the English language."

It is this writer's opinion that the quality of some of Lindsay's verse is high, and, though not as high as Edger Lee Masters thought, it is certainly superior to the verse of Sandburg and superior to the verse of Masters also. Edwin Arlington Robinson offered this assessment of Lindsay's performance:

> Lindsay's work will live for a long time; for there is nothing else like it, and the best of it has a spontaneity and a mark of the inevitable that comes only by what we have to call genius.

Lindsay's apparent spontaneity and simplicity were achieved by the capacity for taking pains, for, as we have noted, he re-wrote a poem as often as fifty times. He also used discretion when dealing with "the language of the common man." Lindsay sang of the people, and for the people, but, for the most part, he worked as a literary sophisticate, well-grounded in the rich soil of English verse, and with the fervor of the dedicated poet. Fortunately, because he had the ability to absorb his sources, they were rarely apparent in his work.

Nor was Lindsay as naïve as some of his critics thought him to be. It must be remembered that he had read Chinese and Hindu writings, and also that, for a period, he had been a Buddhist. In addition he was not only a student of Greek civilization, but his hobby was Egyptian hieroglyphics. It was Lindsay's peasant appearance, his unpressed clothing, his blatant poetry recitals, plus the unruly forelock he affected, which gave him the appearance of naïvete. But this posture did serve to emphasize that he was of the people and that he addressed himself to the people. His programs were designed to recreate the uncomplicated and happy existence "the people's" ancestors had known before the industrialism of the East, the steel ribbons of the railroad, and the insidious Banks had destroyed their Jacksonian Eden. Lindsay wanted the people to live in small villages, close to Nature, to farm, to live by the sweat of the brow, and to enjoy the fruits of their labor. Cities, sky-scrapers, technological advances, middle-men, bankers, indus-trialists, politicians—these stifled the human heart, enslaved the people and involved them in imperialist wars.

Thus Lindsay's message was quite comprehensible and, given his background and character, it was perfectly rational. That the sociologist, the economist, and the politician would dismiss it as impractical, and as a dream of Utopia which could never be translated into reality, is unimportant as far as Lind-say is concerned, for he was incapable of accepting their type of reasoning. He saw industrialism, militarism and the metrop-olis as instruments of reaction. By creating these instruments modern man had provided for himself a corrupting and stulti-fying environment. Quite logically, Lindsay devoted himself to a crusade which would make the people aware that the blandishments and seductions of cities were fatal, and that material progress was meaningless. He was, therefore, equally logical in proclaiming that the wholesome and healthy life was the agricultural life of their forefathers.

His innate optimism saved him from that despair which had such a poisonous flowering in Naziism and Fascism. His re-ligiosity preserved his faith in the "salvation" of man, and also prevented him from accepting any philosophy which regarded the human being as at the mercy of a historical dialectic or as the helpless victim of cultural cycles. At the same time, because of his hostility to technology, he attached no impor-tance to the fact that, in his own lifetime science was providing man with the means to lift himself above poverty, ignorance, and the slavery of tedious and repetitive labor.

Thus, unable to look forward to the future which was taking shape in his lifetime, Lindsay looked backward to the gilded Jeffersonian America of his imagination. He longed for a revo-lution, the type of revolution which G. K. Chesterton described as a restoration. Had such a revolution been possible, and had it taken place, it would have restored the type of America over which the Populists had grieved and which they had bent their efforts to establish.

Chapter VII

CARL SANDBURG

Galesburg and Chicago

Carl Sandburg's *Complete Poems* contains no poems on Populism, no mention of Byran, no attack on Hamilton; and the names of Jefferson and Jackson appear but rarely. Moreover, occasional poems such as "Nocturne in a Deserted Brickyard" and "Prayers of Steel" seem to lend support to the thesis that Sandburg is truly the poet of modern industrialism. Yet there is ample evidence, without recourse to the Populistic panegyric *par excellence, The People, Yes,* that *Complete Poems,* either in itself, or as part of Sandburg's literary production, betrays the pattern of an agrarian sympathizer very much influenced by Populism. There are noticeable variations in the pattern, to be sure; but the pattern is there, and, basically, it differs little from the one found in Edgar Lee Masters and Vachel Lindsay.

Corresponding to Petersburg and Springfield was Galesburg, Illinois, a Republican "horse and buggy" town "within the orbit of the Lincoln tradition," where "the men knew their horses and the horses knew their men," where "the fellowship between horses and men was every day and hour a living reality." The pitchfork was the "tool natural" in the calloused hands of the people of this segment of agricultural America, which, even during Sandburg's boyhood, numbered among its inhabitants pioneers "hard bitten, grizzled, and fading," in their seventies and eighties, who had "broken the prairie, laid the first roads

123

and streets, built the first schools and churches, colored the traditions of the town and country where I was born and raised."

One of the foreign born in this setting was August Johnson, an illiterate railroad worker, who worked a six-day week, ten hours a day, for fourteen cents an hour. This "peon to the railroad," one of the many "Johnsons" hired by "the damned slave drivers," once received the wrong pay envelope and forthwith he changed his name to Sandburg. Thus Carl Sandburg could neither trace his forebears back to the Revolution, nor call his name his own, nor take a pride in his genealogy.

> I may be a Sturm, but to the best of my belief I am a Danielson come to Judgment. I don't wonder genealogy is a racket and the genealogy room at the Library of Congress is always packed with pedigree seekers.

Thus, according to the xenophobic theme of *The New Spoon River*, Carl Sandburg could be classified as a part of the mongrelization of the pristine Republic. He was a hybrid, partaking of the "Viking virtues," as Malcolm Cowley has insisted, and of the plain Midwest, the small town, the prairie soil and wind, the cornfield and the corner barbershop. As such, he was both an "outsider" and a nativeborn American, a contradiction common to most of the minority groups constituting non-Anglo-Saxon America:

> There were names us kids liked to use. We liked them mostly because they sounded funny. A Jew was a "Sheeney." The Irish were "micks." A Swede was a "snorky." A Yankee was a "skinflint." The Germans were "Dutch." The Italians were "dagoes." A Negro was a "nigger" or "a smoke." . . . We believed that the "sheenies" on the quiet might be calling us "snorkies" and calling the Irish "micks" and that would be all right with us because we were. But if they called us "goddam snorkies" or "goddam micks" then we would look for bricks to heave.

The experience of the wrong pay envelope, serving to illustrate the facelessness of a "Johnson," was trivial compared to what was to happen to the August Sandburg, whom Carl has described with pity and indignation:

> As I look back I have regrets and wishes about my father. I regret that my father had a fear of want, a dread in his blood and brain that "the rainy day" might come and in fair weather he hadn't prepared for it. He aimed to be a "good provider." . . . As the years passed there came by slow growth layers of muscle making a lump on his right shoulder. He was day on day swinging sledges and hammers on hot iron on an anvil. . . . We saw him many an evening come home after the ten-hour day, his shirt soaked with sweat, and he had no word nor murmur though he looked fagged and worn.

August Sandburg managed to save sufficient money from his meager income to buy a house. In this achievement he felt the pride of possession and of providing for his wife and seven children, often speaking of his new acquisition as "a nice piece of proputty." Unfortunately, like the Receks, whom Masters defended, the illiterate Swede was chagrined to discover himself the victim of a legal swindle. There was something wrong with the deed, some tricky legality about his possession of the property. He was allowed to keep the house, but he was compelled to pay for it a second time. This incident provided the basis of Carl Sandburg's hatred of "finance." He recalled bitterly:

> Probably there was quoted *Caveat emptor* . . . along with "Ignorance of the law excuses no one." A Swedish emigrant blacksmith "helper" earning a dollar and forty cents a day should beware when buying real estate, and if he is ignorant of the law that doesn't excuse him. Can any degree of guilt attach to those who by their pleas and actions laid all blame, penalties and extractions on a

125

workingman trying by hard work and thrift to own a house and lot in free America?

As Carl Sandburg's biographer has recorded: "The impression this whole unhappy incident made on Carl Sandburg, the small child, has never been erased." Harry Hansen, who knew Sandburg well, has concurred:

> Once the youth of this man is unveiled we realize how deeply his earliest experiences have colored his whole life. It explains his themes, his point of view, his intensity, his compassion and pity.

Part of Sandburg's youth was an awareness of economics and poverty. In his autobiography he has described a background of Coxey's Army in the news for months, men out of work marching on Washington, the Panic, hard times reaching Galesburg. His father's ten-hour day was cut to a four-hour day and the Sandburgs knew hunger in agricultural America: "We learned to eat bread spread with lard, sprinkled with salt, and we liked it."

Politics likewise affected him at an early age, for he saw them "run hot in the blood of men" at a Republican rally. On the way home from the rally, he asked his father questions; and the latter, ignorant of the issues and very likely wanting "to belong" in Republican Galesburg, instilled in the boy the idea that Republicans were good men and Democrats

> good men gone wrong or sort of dumb. And I had a feeling that Cleveland was an ugly man, ugly as you can think of, and if the Republicans got a rope and hanged him I wouldn't be sorry. . . . I was a young Republican, a six-year-old Republican.

At nine years of age, Sandburg was dismissed from school early because of the Haymarket affair. He remembered the satisfaction of an adult passerby who "had the big news of the

day and was glad to spread it . . . 'Well, they hanged 'em!'"
And Sandburg himself believed that the Haymarket rioters
were "not regular people and didn't belong to the human race,
for they seemed more like slimy animals who prowl, sneak, and
kill in the dark."

To offset Sandburg's "Republicanism" there was "Coin" Harvey, town radical and town "character," who spent his time
telling children that the big bankers of America were in a
conspiracy with the Bank of England and that they had put
America on the gold standard, made money scarce, and spread
poverty. The country, Harvey insisted, needed a secret order
of men pledged to keep watch and eventually to take over
the United States Government and run it for the people. With
the control of the government, the first legislation on the program would be unlimited coinage of silver. Carl stood up,
along with "three or four Populists and the rest radical free-
silver Democrats" and took the pledge. In this manner he became a member of a secret society, The Patriots of America.

In 1892, when Altgeld pardoned the three anarchists at
Joliet and issued a statement on the miscarriage of justice
which had prompted his action, Sandburg, as a boy of fourteen, read Altgeld's justification of his action:

> I knew as I moved through that sixteen-thousand-word
> message, crammed with what I took to be sober facts and
> truth, that I wasn't the same boy as five years before
> when I was glad about four men hanged. The feeling
> grew on me that I had been a little crazy, 'off my nut,'
> along with millions of people like myself gone somewhat
> crazy.

Despite the accusations in the newspapers that Altgeld was
himself an anarchist, and undeterred by the chorus of protest
arising from police officers and politicians who in their hate
"couldn't find names nasty enough to call him," Sandburg
formed and maintained a very different opinion. "I leaned
towards him," he wrote, "feeling he was no cheap politician."

127

Thus Sandburg, like Masters and Lindsay, became a partisan of Altgeld. And like both of them he became certain of Altgeld's greatness, "The only governor of Illinois sure to be named by remote generations." Sandburg's more extravagant estimate was to be:

> Altgeld was one of the five Americans noted as having followers who believed they could honestly and without sacrilege compare their sainted figures with Jesus Christ. The others were Abraham Lincoln, Robert E. Lee, John Brown, and Eugene V. Debs.

Inevitably William Jennings Bryan became one of Sandburg's boyhood heroes; he went to see Bryan "get off a train and get on a platform on Mulberry Street next to the Q. tracks and make a speech." Again, when Bryan later spoke in Monmouth, sixteen miles on the Q., Sandburg rode "the cowcatcher of an engine from Galesburg to Monmouth on a cold October night." And while working on a milk wagon Sandburg read Bryan's "Cross-of-Gold" speech. He read it several times, and then all Bryan's speeches on which he could lay his hands. Bryan was "my hero, my Man of the People who spoke for the right and against him were Enemies of the People. He opened his mouth and the words for me that year were truth and gospel." Sandburg's interest in Bryan's campaign of 1896 transcended a mere boyish enthusiasm for politics:

> I enjoyed the fury of the campaign, so much to laugh at or cry over if you like crying. One Chicago newspaper kept after Bryan day on day calling him a "Popocrat," half-Populist and half-Democrat, and I liked the fun of it. When they called him the Boy Orator of the Platte I said that was all right. He was only thirty-five and if he had been a year younger he couldn't have run for President —and he came from Nebraska where the Platte River winds over the prairie. Even when they said his mind was like the Platte River, 'a mile wide and only an inch deep,' I liked it as being smart and funny.

Carl Sandburg became a Bryan Democrat despite the fact that such were in a distinct and unpopular minority in Galesburg. Staunchly Republican August was bewildered by his son's radicalism, certain that "'Sharley' would come to no good end." It was only with maturity that Sandburg realized Bryan was "a voice, an orator, an actor, a singer, and not much of a thinker."

Other sources, besides "Coin" Harvey and Bryan furthered Sandburg's indoctrination into the complex of political ideas we have designated as Populism. The question of pacifism had been brought forcibly to his attention by his uncle Holmes who "voted for Lincoln, but refused to answer Lincoln's call for troops." Victor Lawson's political articles in the Chicago *Record* were daily reading for Sandburg; and Tom Watson's *The People's Party Campaign Book* he read "from cover to cover." Finally, he was influenced by John Sjodin:

> "The 207 big corporations" were running the country, as John saw it, and the time would come when the working people, farmers and labourers, would organize and get political power and take over the big corporations, beginning with the Government ownership of railroads....
>
> I didn't agree with John. I asked him many questions and he nearly always had answers. He believed deeply in a tide of feeling among the masses of the people. This tide would grow and become stronger and in generations to come the American people would challenge and break the power of the corporations, the interests of special privilege. There was no real difference between the Republican and the Democratic parties. Both took money from corporations and did what the corporations wanted done.

John Sjodin favored the People's Party and later became a Socialist, organizing the Galesburg local of the Socialist Party. His main influence, according to Sandburg, was that he inspired Sandburg to take an interest in economic matters.

Sandburg tried to understand the tariff and to picture the "pauper labor of Europe." He wondered whether Europe's cheaply-made goods competing with American production would shut down the American factories, "throw their workers out of work," with the inevitable result that "'grass would grow in the streets.'"

The result of these various influences was predilection for Populist beliefs as the following account of Sandburg at sixteen reveals. He

> talked a long streak to Sam Barrow (a Republican) about the rich being too rich and the poor being too poor, farmers losing their farms on account of mortgages and low prices for their wheat, corn, and cattle, millions of workers in the cities who couldn't get jobs.

Sandburg's unusual interest in politics is but one facet of his structure; he was exposed to all the other influences necessary to shape the agrarian sympathizer and the lamenter for a lost day. In spite of "poverty and worry and hard work," as Karl Detzer has noted, Sandburg's boyhood was a happy one, and a rural one, lacking none of the ingredients for nostalgia. Sandburg had no grandfather such as Squire Davis Masters or Grandpa Frazee, no farm to visit in the summers, yet from a family garden he knew "the feel of carrots as my fingers brushed the black loam off them," and this knowledge was sufficient for Sandburg, the septuagenarian, to assert he had always been a farm boy:

> Why don't I live in Chicago? That's simple . . . I am a country boy. When I wake up in the morning, I've got to be able to see either the prairie or the mountains. . . . When I am in the city I feel like a visitor. . . . I am not certain of myself. I can't think.

Sandburg has described himself in his poetry as a boy with "yellow hair, red scarf and mittens, on the bobsled, in his lunch box a pork sandwich and a V of gooseberry pie." This boy came to know the children and grandchildren of the "pioneers" of Galesburg; and, as in the case of Masters and Lindsay, the pioneers "became real." In addition, this boy of the prairie became an admirer and emulator of Mark Twain and, like Masters, he made his boyhood pilgrimage to Hannibal, Missouri:

> As a lad I had traveled a good deal by freight train. . . . I well remember that one June night in the year 1897, I arrived in Hannibal traveling by freight—my face and hands black from the train dust and soot. I wanted so much to see the boyhood town of my favorite author and that was my only chance of doing so because I was entirely on my own and lacked funds. I never regretted the effort and trouble that it cost me. I say without hesitation that Mark Twain has had a very great influence on my style.

The trip to Hannibal was made during a period in which Sandburg experienced a revulsion for Galesburg: "What come over me in those years 1896 and 1897 wouldn't be easy to tell. I hated my hometown and yet I loved it." As a result Sandburg "drifted"—washing dishes in Denver, working in a construction camp, threshing wheat in Kansas—only to return to Galesburg to learn the "painter's trade." From Galesburg he went to Puerto Rico as an enlisted man in Company C of the Sixth Illinois Volunteers. And this wandering and youthful adventure became for Sandburg "days magically lived," and provided with first hand contact with "the people" and with a simpler, agrarian America.

Sandburg's temporary rootlessness explains his move to Puerto Rico. His wanderings must have made Galesburg seem dull, and his work as a "painter" was neither promising nor congenial. At the same time he saw in the American economic scene no grounds for confidence:

> Newspapers said the country was out of Hard Times, more factory chimneys smoking, the full dinner pail and

the promised McKinley prosperity on the way. Yet there were many men out of work, many men who had left their homes, hoping for jobs somewhere.

It is clear, however, that Sandburg had not as yet thought about the problems of imperialism and war. He certainly did not see in Theodore Roosevelt the demagogue or imperialist denounced by Masters. Apparently he saw Theodore Roosevelt as Lindsay had seen him, as a "friend of the people," for in retrospect Sandburg described him as a "tremendous figure," who "was the first to use the phrase 'malefactors of great wealth'—rich, arrogant, predatory men."

Sandburg spent "five dirty, laborious months in Puerto Rico, making forced marches, fighting vermin and malaria, eating 'embalmed beef,' but fired no shots in anger." He wrote letters from Puerto Rico which were printed in his home-town paper, significant because they mark his journalistic beginnings, and he also acquired a "taste for 'larnin'" from some soldier friend. On his return to America, Sandburg went to West Point, where he "flunked arithmetic and grammar" and was home after two weeks. Despite a later period of pacifism he was "proud of his service in the army" and four decades after the event he wore "a veteran's insignia in his buttonhole." After West Point, "he was given free tuition at Galesburg's Lombard College."

Important during his stay at Lombard College was Sandburg's association with an English professor, Philip Green Wright, who not only encouraged Sandburg in his writing but also printed the pamphlet, *In Reckless Ecstasy*, Sandburg's first work. In addition, Wright wrote the introduction to the pamphlet, taking care to stress Sandburg's proletarian background: "He has seen a great deal of the world; some of it, I believe, from the underside of boxcars, traveling via the Gorky line to literary fame."

In "Invocation" to *Reckless Ecstasy*, Sandburg reinforced Wright's allusion to Gorky: "Give me a stout heart to face entrenched error, and a tender feeling for all the despised, re-

132

jected, and forsaken of mankind," and he expressed his revolutionary sympathies in "Pulse Beats and Pen Strokes":

> For the hovels shall pass and the shackles drop,
> The gods shall tremble and the system fail;
> And the things they will make, with their lives
>   at stake,
> Shall be for the gladness of each and all.

When Sandburg's critics and biographers came to explore his early work, it was the essay entitled "Milville" which claimed their attention. Milville is an industrial hell and, by inference, all cities are hell. As Karl Detzer said:

> He launches into a discussion of labor in the glassworks in those early 1900's pointing out that members of the blowers' union make 5 to 20 dollars a day but that the poor unorganized 'carrying-in boys' must work nine or ten hours for 3 dollars a week. The implication is clear. Workers must organize, labor must present a solid front. In 1904 this was not merely liberal; it was dangerously radical.

Populist influence permeated Sandburg's very first work, in his championing of "the people," and in his echoing one of the major tenets of the cult of the pioneer and farmer—the nobility of work: "Above all other privileges vouchsafed us earthly pilgrims, I place the privilege of work." Nor was this message to suffer any essential change; this first pamphlet clearly indicated all that Sandburg was to express later. As Karl Detzer noticed: "In this book of his college days, Sandburg was trying to say exactly what he said so well thirty-two years later in *The People, Yes.*"

After 1904, Sandburg's journalistic activities continued sporadically. *You and Your Job* (1905), was inspired by a wave of unemployment that was sweeping the state. Then he became interested in Socialism, a movement that was more radical and positive than the Populism of the 1890's. Previously he had shown an inclination for Socialism, and his interest may well have been quickened by developments in Sweden, for even at this time, the country in which his family originated was adopting pro-labor and pacifist policies which carried it far beyond the position reached by the United States. At the same time there was always before him the powerful example of Eugene Debs, whom Sandburg reverenced.

Whatever the influences operative in persuading him to make his decision, Sandburg joined the Socialist-Democratic Party of Chicago without questioning the wisdom or advisability of such a step. He was sent to Milwaukee in 1908 to serve as a party organizer, and in the same year he married a fellow party worker, Lillian Steichen, sister of the famed photographer, Edward Steichen. From 1910 to 1912 Sandburg acted as secretary to the Socialist mayor of Milwaukee. He also worked on *The Milwaukee Daily News, The Milwaukee Leader,* and on *The Day Book,* which was "perhaps America's first tabloid newspaper." These years of political and journalistic activity molded Sandburg into a militant Socialist propagandist. How highly he rated the dissemination of his political principles and opinions becomes apparent when it is known that: "Of his own choice he covered labor news which he found more exciting than riots, murder and fires." Unfortunately, he was never quite able to discard his urge to propagandize. When he turned to *belles lettres,* his art suffered, lacking objectivity. "Truth" and "beauty" could not be treated with detachment, for they were always subordinate to the cause of the working man. Sandburg frankly acknowledged the part which emotion played in his writings: "A man writes the best he can about what moves him deeply."

Sandburg's devotion to the working man also had other origins; he was correcting by overemphasis what he regarded as a bias in the press:

> Perhaps the biggest single thing I learned there was that in the average newspaper there is not a complete suppression of stories the sacred cows don't want printed. But

rather what happens is that the stories get printed with stresses, colorations, and emphases that favor the sacred cows.

After Milwaukee Sandburg secured a position with *System Magazine*. For this publication he wrote such articles as "Muzzling Factory Machines," "Training Workers to be Careful," and "Profits from Waste Space." These articles have a quite unexpected and far from "Socialist" content, and actually give advice to employers on how to run their concerns more profitably and economically. They not only draw attention to the fact that it is in the interests of employers to install safety devices and create good working conditions for their employees, but even remind producers that it pays to advertise. One critic has said that they are "trenchant articles on factory management and various phases of the industrial process," but one can hardly help wondering whether Sandburg, despairing of persuading employers to create safe and congenial working conditions for humanitarian reasons, tried by guile to achieve his ends by appealing to their acquisitive instincts. In any case, these articles are hardly in accord with the rest of his writings.

Burton Rascoe has offered a more acceptable explanation of these articles:

> He has hates, but they are of the abstract social nature.
> . . . When he meets a capitalist his prejudices are dissolved; and about men who had hitherto personified to him greed and cruelty I have heard him, once he had talked with them, say in his august and kindly voice: 'Now, they are pretty good guys when you get right down inside of them.'

In Chicago Sandburg became a member of the "clique," when Harriet Monroe published a considerable body of his verse in her *Poetry: A Magazine of Verse*. His "Chicago Poem" won him the Helen Haire Levinson prize for poetry, a prize which Vachel Lindsay and Edgar Lee Masters also acquired.

He became friends with Edgar Lee Masters, who read his *Spoon River Poems* aloud to him for Sandburg's approval. Sandburg reciprocated when he was ready for book publication by mailing enough poems to Masters to satisfy most publishers in the way of quantity.

The two men had a common cause in their fight for labor. While Masters championed the labor cause in the courtroom during the World War I period, Sandburg, in addition to his journalistic labor bias, was employed for a short time as a "field agent and trouble shooter," in which capacity he interviewed strike leaders and presented their cases in labor papers.

This proved an eventful period for Sandburg, particularly in making important personal contacts and in his "discovery" of Dreiser's novels, which he was persuaded to read by Floyd Dell's book reviews. In addition to introducing himself to Dreiser by letter, he established friendships with Lindsay and William Marion Reedy, and heard Clarence Darrow. Thus Sandburg found himself in a group, each of whose members had been influenced profoundly by Populism, and who, in turn, influenced each other.

An immediate change of attitude, in keeping with the thinking of literary Populists and pacifist Socialists, came over Sandburg as regards World War I. The patriotic veteran of the Spanish American War now insisted that wars are made by despots and are fought by the people:

> A million young workmen straight and
> strong lay stiff on the grass and roads.
> And a million are now under soil
> and their rotting flesh will in the years
> feed roots of roots of blood-red roses.
> God damn the grinning kings, God damn the
> Kaiser and the Czar.
>   "A Million Young Workmen"

Other anti-war sentiments he expressed in such poems as "The Four Brothers," "Buttons," "Ready to Kill," and "Killers." At the end of World War I, Sandburg became interested in the

Communist experiment with its powerfully attractive slogan of Land, Bread, and Peace. In 1918, as a correspondent for the Newspaper Enterprise Association he made a trip to Sweden, where, while in Stockholm, he spent the major part of his time with Per Albin Hanson who at the period was "managing editor of the daily newspaper of the Swedish Social Democratic party." Sweden's Socialist experiment greatly interested Sandburg, and the strong pacifism of the country won his interest and approval. In "Two Sweetheart Dippies," Sandburg made the point that wars are meaningless and that they are fought over nonsensical things. Sandburg remained a pacifist from the end of World War I until 1939. Then, the initial military successes of Hitler, with the threat of world freedom which they implied, caused him to embrace the opinion that some wars are necessary, and he sought justification for militarism in the persons of Washington, John Adams, Jefferson, Lincoln, and Andrew Jackson as leaders who were "fireborn." He broadcast:

> When the war began in 1939 I was for the strictest neutrality. I hoped that France and Britain would in the end win the war, though along with this I had a hope that something might happen to all who had a hand in the strangling of democracy in Czechoslovakia and Spain. . . .

> In other words, I am one of the millions in this country who believe that if we now let Hitler tell us we can't do this or we can't do that, we will later either again let him tell us what we can or can't do—or in that later time we will take the only course open to us, that of fighting a long and bloody war.

All the evils of Wall Street were of less consequence than the totalitarianism of the Axis powers:

> When the question is asked, "Why do you favor the democratic system when it holds so much waste, corrup-

137

tion, demagoguery and other evils?" We answer, "Because we have looked over all the other systems and found that they too have waste, corruption, demagoguery, and other evils, and we take our chance on the democratic system because of what it has that the other systems don't have.

Senator Wheeler of Montana, a latter-day Populist, drew Sandburg's fire for his neutralist speeches:

And how would he mitigate, palliate, this hysteria? By telling it with his open mouth to the country that we have a President of the United States who wants a war that will "plow under" every fourth boy of draft age. By telling it in a nation-wide radio address that the President is under the influence of the international bankers, the Rockefellers and Kuhn Loeb.

Once emotionally involved in any issue Sandburg was rarely capable of any nice discrimination in thought. Like the Orwellian nationalist in general and William Jennings Bryan in particular, he thought "in terms of very black black and very white white." Stalinist Russia, now an ally, became for Sandburg a great champion of mankind. Unlike Dreiser, who discerned the disturbing contradictions in Communist Russia, Sandburg discovered no evil there, or if it won his notice he preferred to remain silent about it.

"The People, Yes"

The striking title poem, "Chicago," of Carl Sandburg's first volume of poetry has served to give him a false reputation as the bard of the city, of industrialism, and of twentieth century commerce. Such lines as:

Hog Butcher of the World
Tool Maker, Stacker of Wheat

Player with Railroads and Nation's
  Freight Handler;
Stormy, husky, brawling,
City of Big Shoulders

have disguised Sandburg's Populistic antagonism toward these very same things and concealed his agrarian outlook. The degree of this error of emphasis is best illustrated by the fact that Harriet Monroe, Sandburg's chief mentor, was not able to grasp Sandburg's essential outlook. In criticizing *Slabs of the Sunburnt West*, Sandburg's fourth volume of poetry, Harriet Monroe still mesmerized by "Chicago," could write

> Perhaps Mr. Sandburg hasn't stayed long enough as yet in the sunburnt Far West. He doesn't feel it as deeply as he does his own Windy City.

Sandburg himself made no secret of his identification with the prairie and the West:

> I was born on the prairie and the milk of its wheat, the red of its clover, the eyes of its women, gave me a song and a slogan.
>
> . . . .
> O prairie mother, I am one of your boys.
> I have loved the prairie as a man with
> a heart shot full of pain over love . . .
> "Prairie"

Nor was this identification a matter of one scattered poem; for Sandburg, like Masters, was a repetitious poet, his mental development fixed to the period of the Populist uprising. We shall proceed to examine then the effects of Populist influence as it appears in his works.

The theme of Sandburg's early "Millville," of industrial ugliness and of sweated labor, was repeated throughout his poetic career, and yet because Sandburg persisted in this theme he has been assumed to be the rhapsodist of *Smoke and Steel*, to cite the title of one of his poetic collections. This is to say that he sees beauty in industry, that the gleaming bands of the railroad tracks are beautiful for him, that the geometric shapes of water towers, storage tanks, pipes, turning wheels, gears are beautiful, that fire and smoke are symbols of man as Prometheus, that the clinks and clanks of the factory, the whirrs of motors are musical harmonies. Such enthusiasms would have to be, and have been, what one could expect of the "poet-laureate of industrialism." However, an examination of scores of Sandburg's poems reveals that such enthusiasms are non-existent. On the contrary, in Sandburg, industrialized twentieth-century America is a hell hole, but it is the people of this milieu who are heroic figures—because Sandburg believed in them with mystic faith. The people manage to exert enormous energies, to be happy, and to be stoical when the occasion demands it, and it is the grace and courage and strength of the people that Sandburg sings of, and not of their cities or their factories.

Studying some of Sandburg's poems to see what, precisely, he does say about urban and industrialized America we find that in "Mill Doors" the people who enter the factory are bled daily drop by drop, and they are old before they are young. In "Halstead Street Car" the pigsticker and the overall factory girl are "tired empty faces . . . Tired of wishes, Empty of dreams." In "Population Drifts":

> One child coughed its lungs away, two more
> have adenoids and can neither talk nor run
> like their mother, one is in jail, two have
> jobs in a box factory.

The same outlook is expressed in "Cripple":

> Once when I saw a cripple
> Gasping slowly his last days with the white
> plague. . . .

I said to myself
I would rather have been a tall sunflower
Living in a country garden.

The city reduces girls to prostitution:

I am the great white way of the city.
When you ask what is my desire, I answer
  'Girls as fresh as country wild flowers.'

All cities, including Chicago, destroy human life:

Of my city the worst that men will ever
say is this:
You took the little children away from the
sun and dew,
. . . you put them between walls
To work, broken and smothered, for bread
and wages.
To eat dust in their throats and die empty-
hearted,
For a little handful of pay on a few Saturday
nights.
                      "They Will Say"

These are not the sentiments of a poet who loves cities, although Sandburg did have moments when cities perplexed
him because of the fascinations they exerted:

I have seen this city in the day and the sun
I have seen this city in the night and the moon . . .
There is something . . . here . . . men die for.
                      "Tangibles"

But since Sandburg wrote no poems to art museums, symphony
halls, theaters, libraries, bookstores, universities—the "city" in-

stitutions expressive of man's spiritual yearning for truth and beauty—we can readily surmise that to Sandburg cities are mere concretions of buildings and masonry, and a herding together of many people.

Like William Jennings Bryan, like Masters, like Lindsay, Sandburg believed that cities are impermanent:

> And the wind shifts
> and the dust on a doorsill shifts
> and even the writing of rat footprints
> tells us nothing, nothing at all
> about the greatest city, the greatest
> nation
> where the strong men listened
> and the women warbled: Nothing like us
> ever was.
>
> "Four Preludes on Playthings of the Wind"

The choice of words and imagery in "rat footprints" is very deliberate, being designed to denigrate the city.

These are hardly the reactions of one who believes in twentieth-century America and in progress. That cities housed "the people" seems to have escaped Sandburg's attention; that the hard floor of cities have nurtured all the progressive and revolutionary ferment of Europe and Asia eludes his notice. The reason for this lack of logical consistency is that Sandburg's heart remained irretrievably fixed on Galesburg and the prairie, both transmogrified by memory. Thus, even when he writes of Chicago, Sandburg's emphasis is on its brutishness, and Sherwood Anderson has rightly characterized this concern of Sandburg's as "the poetry of John Guts."

Sandburg's basic attitude toward New York, the epitome of "the city," cannot be demonstrated to be one of friendliness. Masters, Lindsay, and Dreiser spent many years in New York, but not so Sandburg. As these four men were good friends and as their livelihood depended upon the written word published by New York publishers, Sandburg's absence from New York indicates that he had no liking for that metropolis. He has

142

referred to New York as "a city of many cats" and as "a Babylon," but these statements are at variance with his claim that there is "a rose and gold mist New York." Thus there are no direct means of assessing Sandburg's real feelings about this city, and, in their absence, his attitude must be assessed by other methods. For example, one of Sandburg's admirers considered New York a place of "literary gangsters" who "ignore or belittle the efforts" of honest poets. Masters made this charge repeatedly and Dreiser concurred in it. *Poetry Magazine* also lent its pages to the charge, and these complaints seem to indicate that this was a common feeling among the litterateurs of Chicago. Sandburg seems to have had no quarrel with his various New York publishers, but his modest sales until the appearance of his Lincoln biography may have made him feel that New York critics neglected the honest poets from the "Corn Belt." Margaret Widdemer, for example, has described Sandburg as, "Striking from time to time a few notes on the mouth organ, with a wonderful effect of human brotherhood which does not quite include the East."

On the topic of the commerce of cities, specifically of Wall Street and financiers in general, Sandburg was very articulate. On the whole his concept of them is at one with the Socialist and Communist stereotype. Wall Street "operators" are men who "own a judge or two"; they are "rare and suave swine who pay the stockholders nothing"; they are men who extend their allegiance to any flag which pays its bills and meets the interest on loans. They are a privileged people, being exempt from punishment, and he asserts that they should be compelled, as a class, to enlist for military service. He is ready to believe that bankers succeed in making even more money during lean years, years in which millions of children go to bed hungry every night. In brief, the people connected with high finance are base and dehumanized, isolated from the people:

> What about the munitions and money kings,
> the war lords and international bankers?
> the transportation and credit kings?
> the coal, oil, and the mining kings?

143

the price-fixing monopoly control kings?
Why are they so far from us?
Why do they hold their counsels
without men from the people given a word?

The People, Yes

And because of their vanity and gluttony, those rich by "finance" are to be despised, even in death, and their griefs do not excite the poet's compassion:

Tomb of a millionaire
A multi-millionaire, ladies and gentlemen,
Place of a dead where they spend every year
The usury of twenty-five thousand dollars
For up keep and flowers.

A hundred cash girls want nickels to go to
the movies tonight.

"Graceland"

Take your fill of intimate remorse,
perfumed sorrow,
Over the dead child of a millionaire,
I shall cry over the dead child of a
stock yards hunky.

"The Right to Grief"

In spite of this lifelong hatred of financiers, Sandburg, late in his career, wrote a religious poem to the temple of high finance, the Skyscraper. "Skyscraper Canticle" is a poem of acceptance, and this acceptance raises the question as to the real attitude of Sandburg—that revealed in "Skyscraper Canticle" or the attitude expressed in *The People, Yes*:

Desecrate the landscape with your billboards,
gentlemen,

Let no green valleys meet the beholder's eye
without
Your announcements of gas, oil, beans, soap,
whiskey, beer. . . .

and

What is the story of the railroads, of oil,
steel, copper, aluminum, tire?
Of the utilities of light, heat, power, trans-
port?
What are the balances of pride and shame?
Who took hold of the wilderness and changed it?
Who paid the cost in blood and struggle?
What will the grave and considerate historian
loving humanity and hating no one dead or alive
have to write of wolves and people?

"Skyscraper Canticle," it seems reasonable to assume, is characteristic of peace-making with man and God, common to
many poets in their twilight, rather than the expression of an
enduring attitude.

Of his poem, "Prairie," which we have noted, Sandburg
recorded: "I wrote and rewrote 'Prairie' . . . fourteen times
before it was ready for print." This, in Sandburg's case, was a
labor transcending love and expressing the mysticism of the
agrarian. And with his "Prairie" poem Sandburg paralleled the
experience of Lindsay. It "brought requests for lecture dates
from Corn Belt villages."

Unlike cities, the prairie is eternal and sustaining both life
and death:

I am here when the cities are gone.
I am here before the cities come.
I nourished the lonely men on horses.
I will keep the laughing men who ride iron.
I am dust of men.

"Prairie"

145

And the prairie permeates Sandburg's work, poem after poem being saturated with it. Of the many examples mention need only be made of "Buffalo Dusk," "Improved Farmland," "Buffalo Bill," "Prairie Waters by Night," "Early Moon," "Autumn Movement," "Laughing Corn," "Falltime," "Illinois Farmer," and "Young Bullfrogs."

The prairie is so dominative in Sandburg's volumes that it is impossible to evaluate Sandburg without introducing the prairie and, by extension, the farmland. *Cornhuskers* (1918) is a Sandburg title which speaks for itself. *Slab of the Sunburnt West*, as Howard Mumford Jones pointed out, is largely devoted to "the monumental bigness and fecundity of the central states." The section of Sandburg's *Complete Poems* entitled *Good Morning, America* (1928) is a reminder that "the noise of modern cities cannot dull the poet's ears to songs of birds, prairie winds, and that city streets cannot make him forget the beauty of stars and flowers." Even Harriet Monroe, who defined *Chicago Poems* as an "urban book," qualified this by stating that throughout the volume the controlling motive is "love of the prairie towns and city, and the people who struggle through toilsome lives there." Finally, when writing of the man he worshiped, Lincoln, Sandburg significantly subtitled Lincoln's formative period, *The Prairie Years*, closing his great work with the line: "The prairie years, the war years were over." Consequently this identification of Sandburg with the prairie cannot be overstressed because it has been frequently overlooked or not adequately emphasized.

One need only take note of the diction, the tone, and the thought in Sandburg's many references to the prairie, to the village, to the farmlands, to the people of the farmlands to see how thoroughly agrarian Sandburg was. In numerical count his agrarian and nature poems far outnumber his poems of the city, and even in the latter he frequently uses nature images. For example, in stark contrast with their maimed, disease-ridden end, the people who come new to the city, the prairie people, are beautiful, healthy and vigorous:

New-Mown hay and wind of the plain made her a
woman whose ribs had the power of the hills in them and
her hands were tough for work and there was passion for
life in her womb.

"Population Drifts"

In utter contrast with the hopeless and tired factory workers
of the city is a plowboy presented in sentimental chiaroscuro:

I shall remember you long.
Plowboy and horses against the sky in shadow.
I shall remember you and the picture
You made for me,
Turning the turf in the dusk
And haze of an April gloaming.

"Plowboy"

And in his prose Sandburg often reiterated the idea that the
farmlands were so beautiful they gave him physical pangs:

It was in these fields out near town we saw timothy hay
growing and oats and wheat. Ever since when I meet a
field of them I speak to them as old friends. It is as Indian
corn that hit me deepest

In conclusion, Sandburg was in complete agreement with
both Masters and Lindsay in his attitude toward pioneers,
farmers, and small towns. He wrote a poem echoing Lindsay's
theme that the pioneers are followed by the traders "furtive
and tame," but Sandburg's language and emotions were generally stronger than those of the mild-mannered Lindsay:

First come the pioneers, lean, hungry,
    fierce, dirty . . .
Then the fat years arrive when fat drips.

Then come the rich men baffled by their
    riches . . .
"feed, oh pigs, feed, oh swine."
The People, Yes

And comparable to Masters' Lucinda Matlock was Sandburg's Mildred Klinghofer, under the transparent disguise of
a Teutonic name:

Mildred Klinghofer whirled through youth
in bloom.
One baby came and was taken away, another
came and was taken away.
From her windows she saw the commons young
and green.
And later . . .
In her middle forties her first husband died.
In her middle sixties her second husband died.
In her middle seventies her third husband died.
And she died at mid-eighty with her fourth
husband at her bedside. . . .

Mildred Klinghofer has deep within her "a child hunger." On
her deathbed she is given a doll, "And she was satisfied and her
second childhood ended like her first." Jack is her pioneer
counterpart, in an industrialized society:

Jack was a swarthy, swaggering son-of-a-gun
He worked, thirty years on the railroad, ten
hours a day, and his hands were tougher than
sole leather.
He married a tough woman, and they had eight
children . . .
He died in a poorhouse.

This compressed history with the unexpected ending Sandburg
took straight from Masters. Indeed, in these vignettes, it is not
so much the comparative lack of cynicism which distinguishes

148

Sandburg and Masters as his longer poetic line. But there the comparison ends, for Sandburg was the "Populist" *par excellence*. He sang of "the people," whether native born American or not.

In Sandburg's canon the later immigrant is not responsible for the decline and the decay of the Republic. If anything, the immigrant who is virile and fearless, with an immense capacity for happiness, replaces the pioneer. In "Happiness," Sandburg wrote of Hungarians and their accordions, in "Near Keokuk" of Greeks, shoveling gravel and telling smutty stories; in "The Shovel Man" of the "dago" working for "a dollar and six bits a day."

The strange languages of the immigrants struck a discordant note with Masters, but they aroused in Sandburg a very different reaction. The voices of Italian children quarreling appealed to him as pleasantly as the accordion music of the Hungarians: "I could sleep to their musical threats and accusations." ("Clinton South of Polk"). And, when noting that in Illinois the native stocks were to be outnumbered, Sandburg expressed no concern, being content to record the fact without comment:

> Yes, Illinois was changing. What was ahead in politics no man could tell. The one sure thing was that the people of Kentucky, Tennessee, and Virginia and the Carolinas who had controlled Illinois, were to be outnumbered and outvoted at some time in the near future.

Throughout his life, Sandburg betrayed no taint of anti-Semitism. "Fish Crier" portrays a Jew with all the objectivity of which Sandburg was capable, and while in his Lincoln biography he dutifully records that General Grant excluded "all Jews from his military department," he also draws attention in *The People, Yes* to a Chicago Jew who gave millions of dollars to schools in the South, and who confessed to another Jew, "I'm ashamed to have so much money."

Sandburg's democracy and sense of brotherhood, which excluded only the wealthy, were such that the racism of the

Nazis caused him to prefer the Communists to them and to their Middle-Western "America First" sympathizers. An avowed propagandist, he sought to offset the canard that Jews are cowards by reminding his readers that:

> Barney Ross, the battling Jew who held three prize-ring championships enlisted in the Marines overage . . . took three wounds at Guadalcanal and arriving at West-coast American soil went on his knees and kissed the ground of his country—Ross said it wasn't patriotism; it was something in his heart beyond words.

At one with his democratic principles was his confidence in Asiatics when he predicted that the Americanized Japanese would acquit themselves honorably in World War II. He rejected the notion of "Asiatic hordes," stating: "My prayers go with his (i.e. Maurice Hindus') for the Russian people. If they are merely 'Asiatic hordes,' then I am a barrel-house bum."

Sandburg devoted considerable thought and energy to the Negro question. At the close of World War I, a colored boy crossed an imaginary segregation line in the Chicago area. White boys reacted by throwing stones at him and knocking him from the raft with the result that he was drowned. When the police refused to arrest the white boys, a race riot ensued, and Sandburg was sent by the *Chicago Daily News* to report on the situation. The outcome was a series of articles which appeared in book form.

The report itself shows that Sandburg exercised sufficient restraint to present a reasonably objective account, but in summing up the situation he left no doubt that his sympathies were with the Negroes involved in the case:

> So on the one hand we have blind lawless government failing to function through policemen ignorant of Lincoln, the Civil War, the Emancipation Proclamation . . . And on the other hand we have a gaunt involuntary poverty from which issues the hoodlum.

Thereafter Sandburg was constantly on the alert for any lowering of the color bar, and when one of the "big leagues" was about to try out Negro ballplayers, Sandburg reported it. When he felt that the American Negro was advancing toward higher level of human dignity he took care to broadcast the news over the radio.

No question arises concerning Sandburg's essential democracy in relation to the equality of men, and in this he never faltered nor did he make exceptions. The people were one and all:

1. I am born in the mob—I die in the mob—
   the same goes for you—
   I don't care who you are.

   "Always the Mob"

2. I ask you: Is not the mob rough as the
   mountains are rough?
   And all things human rise from the mob
   and relapse
   and rise again as rain to the sea.

   "On the Way"

3. The people is Everyman, everybody
   Everybody is you and me and all others
   What everybody says is what we all say.

   The People, Yes

4. There are people so near nothing
   they are everywhere without being seen.
   There are people so eager to be seen
   they nearly always manage to be seen etc.

   "Anywhere and Everywhere People"

The contempt for the mob voiced by Masters and Lindsay finds no echo in Sandburg, even though he recognizes that people are "so whimsical and changeable, so variable in mood and in weather." Sandburg had an irrational confidence in the people and, far from fearing them, he held the unreasonable belief that the people inevitably did the right thing. As individuals, hoboes might be ignorant, taxi-drivers unread, laborers unlearned and clerks unlettered, but apply to them the magical term "people" and estimate them collectively and they became possessed of a quite remarkable wisdom. For Sandburg, it was unthinkable that the people might under any circumstances be their own enemies. Their enemies were to be found elsewhere, and Sandburg dutifully identified them, as he had been influenced to do so by the Populists and muckrakers, as the "millionaires."

Sandburg's emotional democracy displays "the utmost scorn for the faction in America which has tried to rise above the common people." And this scorn was characterized by his disapproval of either language, dress, or thought, which sought to rise above the level of the people. Sandburg himself had failed to cope with formal education, particularly with grammar; and he may or may not have had an inferiority complex where higher learning and books were concerned. But one thing is certain, Sandburg repeatedly uttered "anti-intellectual" sentiments and clung to the belief that folk wisdom and folk ingenuity transcend "book-learning." Of his father he wrote:

> Father could not write his own name, and he read little. ... He was the most versatile craftsman I have ever seen: he could do anything with his hands. In a way he was superior to books.

He wrote acidly of the academic critics,

> We've got a new criticism with cellophane on it. The new criticism. You have got to have a code or imagine to have a code in order to know what the hell the Dark Spirits are writing about. They are proud that the average truck driver on Wabash Avenue can't understand them.

When receiving an honorary doctorate from Lombard College in 1923, Sandburg is quoted as saying concerning academic robes: "Where do I get this Ku Klux regalia?"

Sandburg has maintained this anti-intellectualism through-out his life, despite the fact that he himself was an artist who worked with immense application, taking infinite pains: "He pares down and cuts and polishes his verse with the care and patience of an ancient worker in gold." He recognized no dif-ference in rank between "bum," "hobo," "editor," and "profes-sor." He refused to recognize any pejorative connotations for "hobo" and "bum," since he had been a hobo himself and "hadn't changed much since those days," and he wrote not "for poets, or for critics, or for pedagogues," but for "simple people": "I still favor several simple poems published long ago which continue to have an appeal for simple people." And there is evidence to indicate that he evoked a response in his self-chosen audience. According to one Middle-Western librar-ian:

> An examination of the records in a public library of a large American city disclosed the identity of about one hundred recent readers of Sandburg's poetry. They in the most part have the same street addresses as the characters of Sand-burg's own creation.

In Sandburg's poetry there were no Demeters, Hermeses, and Apollos as there was in Masters', nor was there any scien-tific terminology. Absent, too, are the Egyptian Hieroglyphics, Chinese Nightingales, and Buddhas which found a place in Lindsay's poems. Such subject matter savored too much of "intellectuals" whom Sandburg considered "ineffectuals." In fact such subject matter may have been too poetic. For it seems Sandburg had a fear that the words *poems* and *poetry* might be applied to his own work and that of associate *vers-librists*:

> There are a group of us in the United States, perhaps you would call us a type who are struggling along after a kind of freedom. We are not sure we are writing poetry

And, consistently, Sandburg opposed "poet-laureates": "Let us hope the State of Illinois stays out of the laureate business.

153

The habit of having poets-laureate started with kings and queens."

Sandburg seems to have made it almost a point of honor not to look like a poet, but, instead, like "a Michigan farmer." L. Lader commented:

> Even after his books began to make money, his Spartan simplicity remained. He still wears the same unpressed suits. His shoes always need a shine. His dislike of flashy restaurants and night clubs is almost vehement.

And an anonymous writer said, "He wears lumberman's shirts and, an extreme democrat, invites the family goats to the concert." While Lewis Nichols records of him:

> In a warm room, he peels off his coat; in a truly hot room he would probably peel off his shirt. He does not sit, but slouches being aware of the comfortable fact that the primary function of a desk top is as a rest place for feet.

Finally, this obstinacy in dress persisted throughout Sandburg's career; he refused to dress on occasions when he was honored lest he betray his "one gallus" beginnings. The extent of his clothes and class consciousness can be seen in the fact that he considered gloves "anti-democratic."

Sandburg's exultant faith in the people, wherever they were to be found, has created the hallucination that he was celebrating their industrial surroundings and the machine age in which they lived. Nothing is further from the truth. Sandburg never considered the machine as a means of easing the lot of the very people he loved; if anything the machine made the people physically more degenerate and enslaved them. The cities that housed and fed the machine likewise blighted the people—giving them unutterable weariness, tuberculosis, prostitution. The real happiness was to be found in rural America, in Galesburg, in the past. This is evident in his artistic preoccupation with the World as he would have it—the world of

Jefferson, Jackson and Lincoln, the world of folk song, the world of children's stories in a setting of the prairie, which we will deal with next.

Creation of a Folk Hero

In step with the campaign orators of the People's Party and with most literary Populists of his region, Sandburg spread the gospel that Jefferson, Jackson, and Lincoln represented the American political ideal. Of Jefferson, he wrote:

> The fame of this man can last beyond either mediocre monuments or mistaken judgments. The books holding his speeches, writings, and state papers—there they stand. Cold facts, specific data, speculations and hopes around democracy, the people, the American dream, the Bill of Rights—often he says it with music, in a cadence of words that quietly sing.

Jefferson was a "good farmer" who loved peace, who was a teacher of Lincoln, and who influenced Sandburg on the problem of World War II:

> And yet—for eight years he fought in a war—writing with his own hand the war announcement named The Declaration of Independence, making the Fourth of July a sacred calendar date.

There is a self-evident affinity between Sandburg and Andrew Jackson, and it is surprising that he wrote no poem to him. Since Jackson's two periods as President coincided with Lincoln's "twenties," Sandburg did a considerable amount of research on Jackson in the interests of his Lincoln biography. In spite of these labors, Sandburg restrained himself from any personal comments on Jackson, contenting himself with the single observation that Jackson would not have handled the Civil War as ably as did Lincoln. Apart from that, Jackson

155

appears in the Lincoln volumes as a point in time, and as a reference of honor; i.e., such-and-such a person had served under Jackson.

There is irony in the fact that Masters refused to read Sandburg's *Lincoln*, for Sandburg's purpose in writing the biography was "to take Lincoln away from the religious bigots and professional politicians, and restore him to the common people, to whom he belongs." *The Prairie Years* is an expression of nostalgia for the America of Lincoln's New Salem, and every point Masters made about this period reappears in Sandburg. The story of Lincoln's flatboat touching New Salem is told, and a map of New Salem is included. Johnny Appleseed receives mention; the Ann Rutledge story is told with compassion, and Jack Kelso's fishing with Lincoln is recounted. The Sangamon River, the Sangamon prairie valley, and the Sangamon River volunteers of the Black Hawk War make their appearance. The effect of the whole is that of Masters' pristine Republic with its cult of the pioneer and its mystique of work:

> Abe knew the sleep after long hours of work outdoors, the feeling of simple food changing into blood and muscle as he worked in those young years clearing the timberland for pasture and corn crops, cutting loose the brush, piling it and burning it, splitting rails.

But beyond this nostaglia Sandburg and Masters have barely anything in common in their attitude to Lincoln. Sandburg makes a strong point of Lincoln's anti-imperialistic sentiments regarding the Mexican War, stressing the clarity of Lincoln's thought on this matter.

> His public speeches and his confidential letters to Herndon back home fitted together in all parts, pieces, corners, and dovetails. Behind the war he saw (Democratic) politics.

And it is Douglas, who "spoke for aggressive war against Mexico." To reinforce his charge of imperialism Sandburg quotes the dictum of Frederick the Great, "Take possession

156

first and negotiate afterward," as Douglas' credo. Finally, Sandburg drew attention to a point of which Masters had been unaware or which he had deliberately suppressed: "Douglas knew he had a few trumpets left, and he blew them to mass his cohorts behind Lincoln's maintenance of the Union."

In a like vein Sandburg denied that Lincoln was "money hungry" or dishonest; if anything, Lincoln had too much folk honesty to be a lawyer. Neither did Lincoln benefit financially by representing the railroad. As for war profiteers, Lincoln detested them, wishing "Every one of them had his devilish head shot off." Nor was Lincoln a "bank" man, according to Sandburg; rather he had accepted the advice of Chase and Fessenden, "two Treasury chiefs beyond corruption," that a National Bank was "the most efficient financial establishment for the chaos of the hour."

Sandburg admitted that Lincoln's conduct of the war aroused resentment in large numbers of people of Illinois and that the "draft" was extremely unpopular. Sandburg also acknowledged that there was much pro-Southern sentiment in the "North." In spite of these concessions, Sandburg contested Masters' main contention that the Civil War was unnecessary. He saw Lincoln as a genuine democrat, who "saw personal liberty across wide horizons."

The death of Lincoln affected Sandburg deeply. He had lived with his subject for twenty years, giving to him his energies, thought and affection. His grief finds expression in such a line as: "The body of the Friend of Man lies on its back in the centre of the humble walnut bed."

The divergent attitudes of Sandburg and Masters toward Lincoln find their most vivid expression in their contrasting reactions to his assassin. As we have seen, Masters regarded Booth as a patriot and a lover of liberty. Sandburg, on the other hand, could not disguise his aversion to the man who had slain his hero. In an interview with Cyril Clemens he found some excuse for Booth: "I finally came to the conclusion that he was insane, as his father Junius Booth had been before him." In the Lincoln biography, however, Sandburg could not contain his indignation:

. . . the actor-assassin found that his spectacular theatrical performance in Ford's on the night of April 14 was not appreciated as he had expected. He met among Confederate Loyalists suspicious eyes, questioning tones, looks and faces implying: 'What sort of slimy rat are you? Who can trust the likes of you?'

Even this was not enough. Universally acknowledged as a kindly person, Sandburg made no attempt to conceal his satisfaction at the death of John Wilkes Booth:

For on this morning of April 26, hunted like a wild beast and cornered like a rat and dealt with as though he were truly no more than a rat, John Wilkes Booth met his end.

Ironically, his anger against Booth reflected adversely on the Lincoln biography. Throughout this monumental work he had striven earnestly to maintain the highest possible degree of objectivity by refraining from personal comment, and by quoting documents, letters, diaries and journals at length. Yet, his passions aroused, he brings his work to a close in an idiom that is strongly personal.

Sandburg's treatment of Lincoln is completely consistent. It illustrates the obsession with the superiority of one's own power unit that we have already seen in Masters and Lindsay when dealing with such people as Jefferson, Jackson, Johnny Appleseed, James Whitcomb Riley, William Marion Reedy, the pioneer, and the farmer. It reveals the inability of nationalists to interpret data other than subjectively. Thus, while purporting to write biography and history, Sandburg seals off the world of the agrarian South from all impartial consideration. The South is seen as a slavocracy and Karl Marx is introduced to lend support to this accusation. Nor do Southerners, with the solitary exception of Robert E. Lee, excite Sandburg's admiration. Charles A. Beard has written:

There is a chapter on Jefferson Davis and his government, but orthodox Southerners of the Miss Millie Rutherford school will not like it.

In conclusion, Sandburg's immersion in Lincoln resulted in a partial loss of his own identity. This loss involved no radical changes, for not only was Lincoln a direct descendant of Jefferson and Jackson, but he was also "the folk" incarnate, the folk hero. His ringing words of government of the people, for the people, and by the people; his faith in the basic intelligence of the people were already fundamental in Sandburg's credo. The change in Sandburg became apparent in his looking to Lincoln for guidance in action. What Christ is to the Christian, Lincoln became to Sandburg. "What would Lincoln do?" was the question Sandburg asked before making a decision or adopting a course of action; and above all, he tried to be guided by Lincoln's lack of malice. Finally, as the Lincoln biography brought Sandburg money and honors, Lincoln became a vested interest with Sandburg.

According to L. Lader, it was Sandburg's discovery that there were almost no children's tales colored by American folklore and prairie soil which inspired him to write his children's books, and this same motivation or love explains how Sandburg became immersed in folklore. Like Lindsay, he traveled through the country, lecturing, reading his poetry, playing his guitar, and collecting American folksongs. The folksongs which Sandburg collected, which "impressed him most in his wanderings," consisted of cowboy songs, lumberjack songs, railroad work-gang songs, songs of logging camps, steamboat songs. They are precisely the songs of the pioneer democratic America that Sandburg venerated. And what Sandburg was really attempting was to preserve his version of "a past rapidly dying out"; for Sandburg was suspicious of history, describing it as "a bag of tricks." This contempt arose from his conviction that the history of the historians was a different thing from the events which made up the story of a people or nation.

For Sandburg, democracy had to do with the past and with agrarianism; and although he believed that democracy had waned, he made no concrete proposals as to how it might be restored. Despite his conviction that the people, acting in concert, could achieve desirable and worthwhile ends, he offered no practical suggestions as to how the people are to realize them. This may be explained by his realistic attitude toward the city and toward industrialism, which, unlike Masters, he accepted as permanencies. Finally, despite his adherence to Socialism, it does not seem to have inspired in Sandburg any great hope of the morrow. On the contrary, his works betray the profound nostalgia of "literary" Populism.

Glimpses of the nostalgia appear in Sandburg's poetry, obvious examples being "Plowboy," "Village in Late Summer," and "Prairie." But this nostalgia is not limited to a poem or two; it is a consistent thread throughout all his work. Karl Detzer revealed a correct understanding of this abiding sentiment when he wrote:

> All through his writings, even in his most bitter passages, we see him soften when his mind goes to his Illinois boyhood. . . . He paints nostalgic pictures, as when he described himself in 'Prairie.'

Further evidences of this nostaglia appear in *Lincoln, The Prairie Years*, as mentioned previously. Here historical fact was so scanty that it allowed Sandburg to use his imagination with a fair degree of freedom, and while he set out intent on serving American art, poetry, and human behavior by stressing the fifty-two years of Lincoln's life prior to his presidency, Sandburg also wrote a nostalgic requiem to the past—the result was not only the "economic history of an era" finely presented, but was also, as Robert E. Sherwood has said, lyrical prose.

Sandburg's next major venture in nostalgia occurred in the third section of *Remembrance Rock* (1948), a title that has obvious significance. Sandburg intended this novel to be

> an epic, weaving the mystery of the American Dream with the costly toil and bloody struggle that have gone to keep alive and carry further that Dream.

In *Remembrance Rock*, Sandburg was following Masters, in his efforts to show the development of the Republic from

160

George Washington to Harry Truman. The third section of this book has a Middle-Western setting of the 1850's and the Civil War period. As in Masters, the characters sit around discussing politics and economics at length—the views of Sandburg predominating.

An examination of Sandburg's autobiography reveals this ever-present yearning for the past. *Always the Young Strangers* appeared almost two decades after *Across Spoon River*; yet it is apparent that the two men are very similar in their outlook and in their motivations. Sandburg, as his autobiography reveals, never really left Galesburg, no more so than Masters did Petersburg or Lindsay Springfield. In fact, the history of Galesburg is given the same importance as the incidents of his own life:

> I've never written anything quite like it . . . I was trying to get the life of a town and a community, something of the life of a nation. If it should be called anything, it is the biography of a town as filtered through the life of a boy.

Significant also is, as one reviewer has pointed out, that Sandburg seemed "to remember every playmate, neighbor, and town character of the first twenty years of his life."

As Sandburg became a national literary "monument," through sheer longevity, he yielded completely to the past in his newspaper and magazine interviews. At a dinner given to celebrate his 75th birthday he recalled his prairie boyhood and sang folk songs. Age and success had transformed him into "the one living man whose life epitomize the American dream," just as the reviews of his final works frequently emphasized "the American dream." When *Newsweek* made its annual gesture to culture, with Sandburg's picture on the cover, its anonymous writer fell in step: "Sandburg's life itself symbolizes for many that peculiarly American dream of great achievement from humble beginnings." Thus Sandburg has ended by becoming a living example of the sweet agrarian folk type that literary Populism extolled.

Conclusion

As we have seen, there is ample evidence to establish the fact that Sandburg was strongly influenced by Populism. In this respect his life reveals no inconsistency; he wrote of the people, for the people, and in the language of the people. His heroes were Jefferson, Jackson, Lincoln and Altgeld, champions of the people. His theme was that the people, oppressed for centuries, must be allowed to share the fruits of their toil, must be provided with an environment in which toil is possible, and an environment which is productive of happiness. This environment is not that of the cities, or of the factories, and Sandburg, in spite of his Socialism, did not look to the machine and technical progress to free the people from their burden of labor nor even to improve their living standards.

Like Lindsay, Sandburg never sang a thanksgiving to industrial progress. On the whole he was hostile to cities and to industrialization, on occasion without being aware of the fact. Actually he mourned the passing of the frontier as much as did Masters and Lindsay, in *The People, Yes*, expressing his regret with a touch of bitterness:

> Once there was a frontier. Year by year it moved west. At last it moved into the Pacific Ocean. Word passed, 'The frontier is gone, there is no frontier any more.' From then on no more frontiersmen, from then only jokers advising, 'Go west, young man.'

Unlike Lindsay, Sandburg never acknowledged the value of those institutions which preserve the arts of the past, nor did he recognize the value of the past nor the continuity of culture. For him the world was limited in time from around the birth of Jefferson to the death of Lincoln, and in space to the region which had its center in the Middle-West, on the Illinois prairie. Sandburg remained in this place and period throughout most of his life, emulating in dress, speech, and manners as much as possible the rough frontiersman. This strict provincialism excluded from his writings the influences

162

of India, of Greece, and of Europe. He could not, as a "reading man," have been ignorant of these civilizations. It was simply that they were powerless to breach his obsession with the Middle-West.

Where "the people" were concerned, Sandburg had the faith and irrationality of a mystic. The people were wise; the people could do no wrong; the people must inevitaby triumph over those who oppressed and expoited them. Sandburg restricted "the people" to those who worked with their hands. Kings, politicians, priests, bankers, intellectuals, militarists and millionaires were somehow excluded from the rank of "people," because they did not "work." American millionaires and captains of industry were "swine" and "wolves." On the other hand, members of oppressed minority groups or of oppressed nations, whether they were Englishmen, Frenchmen, Spanish Loyalists, Slavs, Chinese, or Negroes belonged to the brotherhood of man. This was an emotional "Populism" which transcended racial differences, historical differences, differences of civilization and culture.

Sandburg never considered the possibility that the people might be stupid or cowardly or predatory or vicious. Here, as in so many other respects, Sandburg differs from the orthodox Socialist. He believed in "the people" as they were, and there is no hint that a new order of society could possibly mean a superior type of person. Nor does he display any faith in historical processes, but with a remarkable ingenuousness, he divided the world into the "good" and the "bad," and it is highly indicative of his mental processes that he never saw reason to revise his evaluation. In his writing, Sandburg's sympathies, which ran out spontaneously to "labor" and the "workers," suffered an insurmountable check when he turned his attention to the individual; and it is not too much to say that he was, with his pen, incapable of isolating the individual from the group. In his Lincoln biography he achieved individualization only by presenting an overwhelming mass of quotation, and, this apart, he failed consistently to achieve personal delineation either in his full-length portraits or in his vignettes. This failure has been noted by several of his critics. Stuart P.

Sherman complained: "He seldom individualizes his working man." William Carlos Williams has described his characters as, "a drift of people, a nameless people for the most part," adding that they "are sand, giving the wind form in themselves until they lie piled up filling his pages."

This lack of discrimination and analysis, which ranks Sandburg as intellectually inferior to Masters and Lindsay, extended to his diction. For even though his poetry was a direct answer to Whitman's hope of a democratic poetry, expressing itself in a distinctively American speech, Sandburg went to extremes. In an excessive determination to avoid affectation Sandburg frequently wrote slang, "tons of it"; and he merited the criticism of being "diffuse, clownish or vulgar, babbling cheap journalese." Even worse, the poetry he wrote for the understanding of truck drivers is too often nothing more than "talk," talk too peculiar to one American economic group to have any universal significance or beauty. Nevertheless this talk was thoroughly Populistic in its vocabulary, in its lack of grammar, and in its content. It was pure Middle-Western and could not have been written in any other part of America, or in any part of the world, or in any other period in history.

Finally, in any assessment of Sandburg's literary stature, it is necessary to separate Sandburg the social reporter from Sandburg the artist. Happily, much of Sandburg the artist and the scholar is evident in his Lincoln biography, in which he excluded Sandburg the propagandist as far as lay in his power. The final result was a magnificent work on a popular folk hero, Lincoln, by a fellow Illinoian, wholly in sympathy with his subject. And it is this writer's opinion that this folk epic of Lincoln, together with his folk autobiography, *Always the Young Strangers*, are the works of Sandburg which will remain after almost all of Sandburg's "verse" has wilted away.

Chapter VIII

THE SPIRIT OF THE RUSTIC

Jose Ortega y Gasset, who grappled with the problem of the people, of the masses, observed "there are peoples who stay forever in the village stage of evolution. They occupy enormous areas, but their spirit is always that of the rustic." Such a people were the inhabitants of the American Middle-West, who saw their agrarian way of life threatened by industrialism and immigration. Their immediate reactions to the prospect of change were those of fear and resentment, but a series of economic crises galvanized them into action. They created a third-party movement, Populism, the aim of which was to win control of the national government.

Populism was a confusing and contradictory movement. It was eclectic, partaking of anarchism, socialism, communism, and even fascism—all the ideologies which were to develop in twentieth-century Europe. However, Populism was wholly American, something its spokesmen tried to explain to the electorate. It consisted of Jackson's "equal rights for all"; of Lincoln's "labor is prior to capital"; of the later governmental paternalism in the Square Deal, the New Deal, and the Fair Deal; of Jefferson's philosophy that "that government is best which governs least"; and of Thoreau's anarchistic idea "that government is best which governs not at all." This paradox of fierce individualism and statism was never rationalized satisfactorily by the Populist orators and writers.

The defeat of Bryan brought an end to the People's Party as an entity in American politics, but Populism remained, as

Tom Watson had predicted it would, a vital force of protest and reform. Its xenophobia destroyed the League of Nations and bred the McCarran Act and McCarthyism. Many of its demands for equal rights were realized in the form of "progressive" legislation on the national level. For the farmer it won a subsidization at the expense of the whole citizenry. Its prototypes of Jackson and Lincoln set the standard that politicians aspiring to the Presidency appear to be "folksy," and not too intellectual or effete. And finally it influenced three of America's important poets.

In temperament these poets are dissimilar: Masters: pessimistic, even lugubrious; Lindsay: optimistic, childlike, and emotional; Sandburg: mystical and aggressive. Indeed, their poetry reflected these differences: *The Spoon River Anthology* seems to be the work of a village cynic; *General William Booth Enters Heaven* and *The Congo* are collections of poems in which the primitive rhythm of "jazz" is conspicuous; and *Chicago Poems* and *Smoke and Steel* celebrate American energy. Thus, it is not strange that contemporary criticism which has focused its attention on what is unique in each of these poets has failed, for the large part, to appreciate the influence that unites them.

Petersburg, Springfield, and Galesburg, the prairie hometowns of these poets, were a part of agrarian America, Masters' "pristine Republic." And each of these poets lived long enough to witness the transformation of his boyhood milieu. He witnessed also a decadence in men: the pioneer and farmer was replaced by the "Babbitt." Each poet responded similarly to the new America; he could not reconcile himself to it. Yet he could not, like the literary expatriates of the 1920's, escape. He loved his country too much to abandon it. He was to be haunted, tormented, dominated, and inspired to the last by the image of the nation America could be.

From this common background and faithfulness to old gods and shibboleths came a close personal and literary relationship. These poets influenced, imitated, and even plagiarized one another. In many instances they spoke as one man. Their message was that the real America was the America of Jefferson and Jackson, of the frontiersman, of the farmer, and of the hearts of the people. This America's youth was represented by the fictional Tom Sawyer and Huckleberry Finn; its *belle lettres* by Emerson, Thoreau, Whitman, Twain and James Whitcomb Riley; its politics by John P. Altgeld and William Jennings Bryan; its sweet folk types by Johnny Appleseed and Jack Kelso.

They were convinced that the old happiness could be restored only if America could somehow return to its pioneer state. Far from worshiping industrial progress like the ameliorative evolutionists of the nineteenth century, or success, in keeping with the Horatio Alger myth and Social Darwinism of their day, these poets were actively hostile to both. Their agrarian sympathies made them temperamentally unsuited for utopian group ideologies such as socialism and communism, which saw in industrialization the salvation of the common people and their ultimate freedom from uncongenial labor. These poets did not regard labor as penance; rather they saw in toil and sweat a discipline which was in itself good and which produced other worthwhile virtues.

One reason they could not accept the benefits of scientific and technical progress was that there was nothing in their village background to give them guidance. They had been influenced to be concerned with the problems of the farmer and of the countryside. All else stemmed from the city, and they shared the rustic's distrust of and hostility toward the city. For them, the city was a place which corrupted the honest, healthy country folk who came to it. Their own experiences with the sordidness of Chicago (and such articles as "The Shame of Cities") convinced them that big cities were as unnecessary and as ugly as an outcrop of weeds. Being agrarians they knew what to do with weeds. Chicago, a Middle-western variety of weed, they spared; but New York, Philadelphia, and Boston could be eradicated and the countryside would never miss them. Masters wrote of swine cities and the failure of such a people; Lindsay wanted the cities emptied and abandoned; and Sandburg envisioned "the greatest city" leveled and marked with rat footprints.

167

Ironically it was the urban populations who, by their numbers and ability to organize, secured many of the reforms which the Populists had demanded. But these poets were impervious to any reforms which might come from the city. They lived in Chicago and New York most of their lives, without "belonging" to them. Nor was this estrangement occasioned solely by the rustic's dislike of urbanized living, for there came opportunities for them to return to their small towns. Yet they could not do so—permanently.

One reason for this inconsistency is that the America they dreamed of, and to which they longed to return, was not a reality. If this America had ever existed beyond the pages of *Huckleberry Finn* and *Tom Sawyer*, it had vanished before they were born. Their nostalgia was a product of the mythology of "the good old days," which their elders, their neighbors, and the Populist orators had painted for them. Lewistown was a representative small-town of the Middle-West; yet once Masters reached his majority, he did not return to it nor speak kindly of it. On the contrary, he insisted that no American writer had ever been as thwarted by a place, and he chose to idealize Petersburg, where he had lived until the age of ten. On retiring from law, he preferred to live in New York City—visiting Petersburg during an occasional summer. Lindsay, who loved Springfield, was curiously absent from it for long periods of time. In a like vein, when Sandburg had accumulated enough money to choose his place of residence, he did not return to "horse and buggy" Galesburg but bought the estate of a Treasurer of the Confederacy in Flat Rock, North Carolina.

Neither was there anything else in emerging America which could satisfy their rootlessness or their dreams. They could not accept its methods or the things which it was creating; and they were wholly out of sympathy with its values. Money, predominant in capitalism and the goal of "success," was an incentive which had little appeal for them. Whenever money came into their hands, they were careful to avoid the "conspicuous consumption" which testifies to its possession. Their Jacksonian egalitarianism was so thorough that they made a fetish of inexpensive, rumpled, and worn clothing; of unruly

168

locks of hair (Masters was bald); and their hatred of evening clothes and of ostentation (including the cap and gown of the scholar) was obsessive. Sandburg, in fact, thought that gloves were basically undemocratic.

These poets extended their egalitarianism to the intellectual sphere. All three were intellectuals, men of the written word and of ideas; yet they refused to elevate their own calling and the institutions associated with it above those of the people. In fact they had the uneasy feeling they contributed less than the manual worker who did the world's work. Each of them protested that the working man who was skilled with his hands was superior to most men and to books; and they attributed to him a capacity for happiness, for what C. S. Lewis has, in another frame of reference, termed "joy."

Their contribution to the people's "joy" was their poetry. They wrote in an idiom the people could understand, about American themes; and they frequently recited their poems before audiences composed of farmers and laborers. They exhorted the people to shun the gods of materialism; they reminded the people that happiness was to be found in Nature, in honest toil, in play. They painted nostalgic pictures of a vanished America, when the people had not been enslaved by the machine, when the people had not lived stunted and throttled in the hive of the city.

ACKNOWLEDGMENTS

The idea and patient overseeing of this work came from Professor Ernest Earnest of Temple University, who was assisted by Professors Gaylord C. Leroy and William Rossky, two readers who insisted on clarity, in thought and word.

Mrs. Edgar Lee Masters and Nicholas C. Lindsay graciously and generously allowed me to use both published and unpublished materials relating to Edgar Lee Masters and Vachel Lindsay.

Much kindness and assistance was shown to me by the librarians of the Lockwood Memorial Library, University of Buffalo; the University of Chicago Library; the Dartmouth College Library; the Berg Collection, New York Public Library; the Rare Book Collection, University of Pennsylvania; the Reading Public Library, Reading, Pennsylvania; the Mills Memorial Library, Rollins College; the American Literature Collection, University of Southern California; and Temple University Library.

I am indebted to the publishers below who permitted me to quote from works under their imprint. In addition I must acknowledge my gratitude to a score of people whom I have quoted, availing myself of "fair usage." In almost all of these cases credit is given in the text; where it is not given documentation is available by consultation of the original manuscript at University Microfilms, Ann Arbor, Michigan.

From *Carl Sandburg, A Study in Personality*, by Karl Detzer. Copyright © 1941 by Harcourt, Brace and Company, Inc.; and used by their permission.

From *Midwest Portraits* by Harry Hansen, copyright, 1923, by Harcourt, Brace and Company, Inc., renewed 1951, by Harry Hansen. Used by permission of the publishers.

From *Candle in the Cabin* by Vachel Lindsay. Copyright 1926 by D. Appleton & Company. Reprinted by permission of the publishers Appleton-Century-Crofts, Inc.

From *Collected Poems* by Vachel Lindsay. Copyright 1913, 1914, 1916, 1917, 1919, 1920 and 1923 by The Macmillan Company. Reprinted by permission of The Macmillan Company.

From *The Congo and Other Poems* by Vachel Lindsay, Copyright 1924 by The Macmillan Company. Reprinted by permission of The Macmillan Company.

171

172

NOTES

[1] Anne Rochester, *The Populist Movement in the United States* (New York: International Publishers, 1944), p. 52.

[2] Unpublished letter, March 8, 1940, University of Pennsylvania.

[3] Edgar Lee Masters, unpublished letter to Theodore Dreiser, March 17, 1939, University of Pennsylvania.

[4] Unpublished letter to Theodore Dreiser, May 10, 1940, University of Pennsylvania.

[5] Unpublished letter to Theodore Dreiser, February 14, 1939, University of Pennsylvania.

[6] Masters said that he, too, was discriminated against by New York publishers of the Jewish faith. He wrote: "Dear Doctor Dreiser: I am the victim of the anti-Gentile prejudice. I can't get a publisher. . . . These surely are troublous times of a people who are just Americans and have no church or race alliance." Unpublished letter from "Lute Puckett" (Edgar Lee Masters) to Theodore Dreiser, January 13, 1938, University of Pennsylvania. One critic took Masters to task for his anti-Semitism. ". . . and then to find another source of blame in the Jews who became so influential and powerful in the publishing field and who had no interest in the Americanness of the Springfield Poet. Such naiveté on the part of Mr. Masters is not only reprehensible; it is vicious." V. F. Calverton, "Vachel Lindsay; Peddler of Beauty to the Masses," *Modern Monthly*, IX (June, 1936), 28.

In spite of Masters' anti-Semitism, the lawyer he admired most was not only a Jew, but a corporation lawyer. Masters admired him so much that he wrote a full-length biography about him. See *Levy Mayer and the New Industrial Era* (New Haven: Yale University Press, 1927). Here Masters forgot his xenophobia temporarily. He wrote: "I also admired Mr. Mayer for his intense Americanism. Americanism is not a matter of race, tongue or birthplace. Americanism is a spirit. Those who have the spirit of America in their souls and believe in its ideals are Americans of a high order." *Ibid.*, p. 250.

[7] Unpublished letter, March 16, 1939, University of Pennsylvania.

[8] Unpublished letter to George Sylvester Viereck, October 27, 1937, University of Buffalo. In this letter Masters also claims that Wilson dishonored Bryan "who made him, who made the day and the movement which lifted him to power." In the same letter, Masters wrote: "I dis-

trusted Wilson when he first appeared on the scene, and refused to come out only for him. My support was negative in 1912. He seemed a lesser evil than Taft and Roosevelt. I was turned against Wilson by his history of the American people." In another letter to Viereck, Masters asserted: "I have always felt that the Kaiser was atrociously libeled, in one of the mob hunts that take the world all the time. I felt this without knowing very much about it." (Unpublished letter, October 23, 1937, University of Buffalo.)

⁹ Unpublished letter to Charles Hanson Towne, June 14, 1938, New York Public Library.

¹⁰ "Mr. Masters was stricken with pneumonia, and a friend who was with him at the time, not knowing what to do, took him to Bellevue Hospital, from which he was sent to a small private hospital. Mr. Masters believes that it was because of this trip to Bellevue that the story arose that he was hungry ad broke. The newspaper failed to print a correct version of the story." "News Note," *Poetry*, XLIV (May, 1944), 116.

¹¹ Unpublished letter, December 15, 1915, Lockwood Memorial Libary, University of Buffalo.

¹² Unpublished letter, September 22, 1915, Lockwood Memorial Library, University of Buffalo.

¹³ Letter to A. Joseph Armstrong dated October 10, 1921. Lindsay's letters to Armstrong were reprinted in *The Baylor Bulletin*, [Baylor University, Waco, Texas], XLIII (September, 1949), 1-121.

¹⁴ Unpublished letter to Louis Untermeyer, December 21, 1917, Lockwood Memorial Library, University of Buffalo.

¹⁵ Unpublished letter to Louis Untermeyer, January 25, 1920, Lockwood Memorial Library, University of Buffalo.

¹⁶ Unpublished letter to Louis Untermeyer, March 31, 1917, Lockwood Memorial Library, University of Buffalo.

¹⁷ Unpublished letter to Louis and Jean Untermeyer, January 1, 1920, Lockwood Memorial Library, University of Buffalo.

¹⁸ Unpublished letter to Louis Untermeyer, December 11, 1920, Lockwood Memorial Library, University of Buffalo. J. C. Squire was the editor of the very important *London Mercury*. He had "spread Lindsay's poem on Bryan over six and a half of its ample pages and gave its readers enough to sit up for days thereafter." "Vachel Lindsay in London," *The Literary Digest*, LXV (May 15, 1920), 43.

¹⁹ "A Letter of Vachel Lindsay on the 'Movies,'" July 24, 1916. Privately printed by Nathan Van Patten. Reserve Book Room, New York Public Library.

²⁰ Unpublished letter to Louis Untermeyer, November 29, 1914, Lockood Memorial Library, University of Buffalo.

²¹ Unpublished letter to Louis Untermeyer, December 28, 1917, Lockwood Memorial Library, University of Buffalo.

²² *Ibid.*, July 25. 1915.

[23] Unpublished letter to Louis Untermeyer, Lockwood Memorial Library, University of Buffalo.

[24] Unpublished letter to Louis Untermeyer, December 21, 1917, Lockwood Memorial Library, University of Buffalo.

[25] Unpublished letter to Katherine Lee Bates, November 5, 1923, Berg Collection, New York Public Library.

[26] Unpublished letter to Louis Untermeyer, January, 9, 1920, Lockwood Memorial Library, University of Buffalo.

[27] *Ibid.*

[28] *Ibid.*

[29] Unpublished letter to Louis Untermeyer, November 28, 1914, Lockwood Memorial Library, University of Buffalo.

[30] Unpublished letter to Louis Untermeyer, December 21, 1917, University of Buffalo.

[31] Unpublished letter, November 25, 1914, Rollins College.

[32] Unpublished letter, August, 20, 1912, Dartmouth College Library.

[33] Unpublished letter, October 27, 1913, Manuscript Division, New York Public Library.

[34] Unpublished letters to Louis Untermeyer, December, 16, 1915, December 21, 1917, January 1, 1920, Lockwood Memorial Library, University of Buffalo.

[35] Unpublished letter, December, 1920; Lockwood Memorial Library, University of Buffalo.